Dual Identities:

Counseling chemically dependent gay men and lesbians

Dana G. Finnegan, Ph.D., CAC

Emily B. McNally, M.Ed., CAC

First published January, 1987.

Library of Congress Catalog Card Number: 86-082658
ISBN: 0-89486-418-1

Printed in the United States of America.

Editor's Note:
    Hazelden Educational Materials offers a variety of information
on chemical dependency and related areas. Our publications do
not necessarily represent Hazelden or its programs, nor do they
officially speak for any Twelve Step organization.

DEDICATION

We dedicate this book to all those lesbians
and gay men who struggle daily to
overcome the dual oppressions of chemical
dependency and homophobia.

CONTENTS

FOREWORD

Summer of 1986 saw New York's largest Gay Pride parade fill Fifth Avenue from noon until well after six. It was led by the mayor and celebrated a City Council decision to pass its long-delayed anti-discrimination bill. The sun was shining, the onlookers almost uniformly friendly or merely curious. The days of hatred, hositility, and bigotry seemed to be ending. Within 48 hours the U.S. Supreme Court announced its refusal to overturn Georgia's sodomy law, a law that defines sodomy to include more activities than its actual definition and dictates the sexual behavior of consenting adults even in the privacy of their bedrooms. We are clearly a long way from consensus. Reason, logic, consistency, and compassion seem sadly missing.

The eighties are also the years when AIDS is forcing its way into national awareness. Circumstance brought it first to the American gay community. (This was not true in Africa where it seems to have originated, or in Haiti where the next major outbreak appeared.) It spread rapidly to intravenous drug users. In New Jersey there are already more new cases among their ranks than among gays and bisexuals. It is moving slowly but steadily into the larger community of those who are not gay, addicted, black, hemophiliac, impoverished migrant workers, or prostitutes. The HIV virus is just that, a virus, not a lifestyle. Just like herpes it strikes at those who are most sexually active. Unlike herpes, it kills adults as readily as it does children. Since it began here with people who are already victims of stigma and discrimination it provides an excuse to increase the witch hunt.

This book is long overdue. There are many good books and articles on chemical dependency and on working with gay and lesbian people. There is woefully little that deals with both subjects together and even less that prepares the reader to think about AIDS. What can present a greater challenge to our

1

attitudes than the fear of contagion, homophobia, and our reluctance to deal honestly with a young person who may be dying when all three of these concerns are wrapped up in one person? Even though these three fears seem unrealistic, that does not make them any less real. And these facts will change little until the emotional mythology that our feelings are based on changes as well.

People in the chemical dependency field are, I believe, uniquely equipped to understand gay and lesbian people. Most of these people are all too aware of what ignorance, prejudice, denial, and stigma do to alcoholics and other addicts. Most have heard the endless discussions about whether or not to "come out" as an alcoholic to friends and family or on a job application. Except for the handful of people who meet the stereotype, the sober alcoholic and the gay person are equally invisible unless they choose to reveal themselves. They are present among us in almost identical numbers. Everyone knows some of them. Almost every family includes them. Many of the less aware deny this and are sincerely and thoroughly blind.

There is one major difference between the two groups. While each is usually misinformed about the nature of the condition and has been schooled to deny the truth or to admit it only with shame and guilt, recovery for the chemically dependent person usually begins with an acknowledgment that he or she is ill. With the gay and lesbian, recovery begins with learning that he or she is not ill.

Just as people who have not experienced addictive illness can learn to work effectively with the chemically dependent, they can also learn to work with gays and lesbians without sharing their orientation. Neither task can be approached with ignorance. Those who can read this book with open minds and hearts will be off to an excellent start.

LeClair Bissell, M.D.
New York City
Fall 1986

2

FOREWORD

Lesbian and gay alcoholism treatment has evolved rapidly as a field of study in the past decade, yet only a handful of books that address the subject have been published. This text contributes greatly in furnishing alcoholism providers with practical approaches and ways of thinking about and counseling this very large group of alcoholics. Even though it focuses on the specific needs of gay male and lesbian alcoholics, the familiar bottom line alcoholism counseling techniques are integrated with specific measures for successful intervention with this often invisible group of clients.

The authors have outlined an important paradigm for identity formation in understanding the process of change experienced by both alcoholism agencies and counselors themselves. One maxim states that when gay individuals "come out" to their families, these family systems experience a change. This same kind of dynamic interchange occurs within treatment agencies when "new" subgroups become apparent as needing alcoholism services. The sometimes feared impact of change must be met with an acceptance of a new identity and of new roles. As Finnegan and McNally so concisely and lucidly describe, much the same process is experienced by lesbians and gay men in coming to grips with their "true selves."

Though lesbians and gay men have much in common, mainly related to the pressures of homophobia and to shared social activities, the treatment approach to gay men and women often requires specialized sensitivity, awareness, and individualized techniques. For example, these approaches require the counselor to focus on the shared experience of gay men, yet remain aware that they are not a homogeneous group. Gay men are as different from each other as heterosexual men are. This group cuts across the barriers of race, creed, ethnic background, age, and socioeconomic status. There are, in addition, subgroups within the gay male subculture itself.

3

Among them are professional groups, "leather" groups, "clones," gay "courts," church groups, and many others. Not all gay men identify themselves with the general subculture or any of the specific subcultures. It is imperative that the counselor listen carefully to the client to learn exactly how particular experiences and viewpoints as a gay man or lesbian relate to the alcoholism — just as one would do with the unique experiences of a black alcoholic.

This text, in its wisdom, concentrates mainly on general and attitudinal approaches to therapy with this population. Comprehending the details of a subculture takes time and direct experience and cannot be covered in one volume. Many patterns exist and must be taken into account when utilizing a systems approach to treatment. Gay men, perhaps more than others, fear and believe they cannot achieve satisfactory relationships and may have a heightened fear of loss of independence, particularly if they have only their own previous alcoholic relationships as examples of gay intimacy. Finding, establishing, and maintaining relationships are frequently encountered concerns in recovery. A counselor with knowledge of how and where this is accomplished in a gay male context can greatly improve strategies of support, awareness, and advice.

Successful alcoholism therapy depends heavily on positive social support. Since the early 1970s, the gay community has developed a vibrant and diverse wellness/health movement. In all large cities a wide variety of gay sober environments exist. Recovery may well depend on awareness and utilization of these resources.

In addition to the frequently encountered emotional difficulties listed in this book (depression, anxiety, guilt, and paranoia), homophobia, both internalized and external, is perhaps the greatest stumbling block in the recovery road for gay men and lesbians. It is well addressed in this text.

Most experienced counselors would agree that the treatment of gay alcoholism depends on concern for the alcoholism first and foremost and for "gayness" second. Taking this one step further, we could say, "We don't treat gay alcoholics nor do we treat alcoholics. We enter into therapeutic relationships with individuals, each with his or her own complexity and uniqueness, and assist them towards sobriety, freedom from other drugs, and a satisfactory life that is true to their, and not our, inner beings."

Tom Mills Smith, M.D.*

---

*Dr. Smith is a recovering alcoholic with over twenty years of experience working with alcoholics. He has been director of the Alcoholism Evaluation and Treatment Center at San Francisco General Hospital, psychiatric consultant to San Francisco's city funded alcoholism programs, clinical consultant to several gay identified alcoholism agencies and groups, and a sex therapist in private practice. He is the author of numerous articles on gay substance abuse, AIDS, and general aspects of alcoholism.

ACKNOWLEDGMENTS

Reaching the point where we could write this book has been a long, difficult, complex, and exciting process; it is impossible to directly thank all of those who have contributed to it. We would like, however, to express our appreciation to those who have played a prominent role in aiding our own growth and development as well as furthering the cause of gay/lesbian liberation and the National Association of Lesbian and Gay Alcoholism Professionals (NALGAP).

We wish to thank all the people, both gay and non-gay, in our Rutgers University courses, our workshops, and our seminars who taught us so much of what is in this book through their questions and sharing.

We thank the administration and staff of the Rutgers Summer School of Alcohol Studies for their courage, concern, and continuing support. They made the course, "Alcoholism Counseling and Sexual Identity Issues," a reality.

We extend our thanks to all those people in the gay/lesbian movement who have helped make the world safe enough for us to do our work — especially the National Gay Health Coalition for their encouragement and recognition of NALGAP's efforts.

We thank the pioneers of the gay/lesbian alcoholism movement whose contributions formed the foundation upon which NALGAP was built. Their example of being out and of being deeply concerned about gay/lesbian alcoholics inspired us and led to the founding of NALGAP.

We thank Jack Ryan, whose dedication and energy have helped enormously in producing the *NALGAP Newsletter*, organizing the Midwest Chapter, leading the national organization of NALGAP, and handling the membership. This book could not have been written without his contributions.

We thank LeClair Bissell, M.D., our editor and friend, who urged us to write this book and didn't give up when we said we were too busy or when we ran into difficulties.

6

We also wish to thank Tom Smith, M.D., whose dedication as a writer, teacher, activist, clinician, and caring person has inspired us and provided us with a model for our own lives.

Finally, we thank our children, families, and friends for their acceptance of us and the contribution of their growth, love, support, laughter, and hugs over the years, especially when life seemed full of problems and stress. They helped us "lighten up!"

INTRODUCTION

We — Emily McNally and Dana Finnegan — came to the writing of this book by very different paths. Although we are both lesbians and recovering alcoholics, we came from very different lives. Emily married and raised three children. When she was three years into recovery from alcoholism, she began to work through her sexual identity issues and to live her life as a lesbian. Dana knew from early in life that she was a lesbian, but did not really come to terms with her sexual orientation until four years after stopping drinking and a few months after stopping all pills. Emily is a Certified Alcoholism Counselor, has a master's degree in psychology, and is a Ph.D. candidate in the Counseling Psychology program at New York University. She is currently writing her dissertation on lesbian recovering alcoholics.

Dana has a Ph.D. in English and taught college level English courses for over ten years. She is a Certified Alcoholism Counselor, has done both general and alcoholism counseling for the past thirteen years, and designed and directed an outpatient alcoholism treatment program at East Orange General Hospital in East Orange, New Jersey, from 1980 to 1985. Currently Emily and Dana are Co-Directors of Discovery Counseling Center, private alcoholism counseling centers in South Orange, New Jersey, and New York City.

We met in 1974 and have lived together since then. Emily's children lived with us for the first three years of our relationship, and they are an important part of our lives. Five years after we met, we attended the 1979 Rutgers Summer School of Alcohol Studies where we "came out" to faculty and fellow students and where, together with other gay men and lesbians, we formed the National Association of Gay Alcoholism Professionals (NAGAP — later renamed NALGAP when the word "lesbian" was added). As Coordinators of the central office of NAGAP during the following five years, we heard from gay men and lesbians all over the country. We received letters and phone calls from gays who had been in treatment or who couldn't get treatment; they told us about their experiences, their fears, their pain, and their isolation. We heard from gay/lesbian A.A. members about conditions around the country. And we heard the concerns of gay/lesbian alcoholism professionals. The most often mentioned issues were the need for raised consciousness, altered attitudes, and more accurate information and knowledge among those who treat gay/lesbian alcoholics.

In addition, we have been active in training and teaching treatment personnel about counseling gay/lesbian alcoholics. For the past five years we have taught a three week course on this subject at the Rutgers Summer School of Alcohol Studies. In this course and in other training sessions, we repeatedly hear concerned people's questions, puzzlement, and their honest desire to learn more and to understand. They want to become more proficient, more comfortable, and more empathetic in their counseling of gay/lesbian alcoholics.

Thus, the material in this book is drawn primarily from our own personal and professional experience. It is also drawn from what we have learned since our own gay/lesbian consciousness has been raised. Because both of us lived a heterosexual lifestyle for many years, we had much to learn and many attitudes to change. We are deeply grateful to those who led the way, who helped light the path ahead of us, who held out the hand of friendship and support, and who taught us by their courage and example how to be "gay, proud, and sober."

Basic Premises

Certain assumptions underlie what we say in this book. Alcoholism is a disease. The only proven way to successfully treat it is by total abstinence from *all* mood-altering chemicals.

We have chosen to use the term *alcoholic* throughout the book rather than the term *chemically dependent*. But we want it to be clear that when we refer to alcoholism we are always referring to *all* chemical dependency.

Gay male and lesbian alcoholics are frequently an unrecognized and underserved population with issues that are special to them and need to be understood and addressed by helping professionals.

There are no easy answers or formulas for the "always do X; but if the client is gay, do Z" variety. There are a lot of questions and some helpful suggestions and guidelines. But much of what is said must be heard with the qualification of "it depends . . . ."

It is important to remember gay men and lesbians are as diverse as alcoholics. Just as we cannot accurately talk about "the" alcoholic but must talk about many different alcoholics, we also cannot accurately talk about "the" gay man or "the" lesbian but must talk about many different gay men and lesbians.

The subject of this book is extremely complex and, of necessity, is presented in a rather simplified manner. It is important to remember any consideration of gay/lesbian alcoholism issues necessarily involves simultaneously examining the interactions among many factors such as sexuality, alcoholism, psychology, physiology, social and religious mores, and cultural attitudes.

Because of this complexity, this book can serve only as a beginning, a guide, and cannot replace experiential training, reading, interacting with gay males and lesbians, and direct counseling experience. Readers will have to secure these experiences for themselves.

This book can provide both information and practical suggestions, guidelines, and techniques.

We write from a wellness perspective, one that views being gay or lesbian as lifestyles which fit within the boundaries of health. Until recently, much of the psychological literature has asserted that to be gay or lesbian was to be mentally (if not also physically) sick. We and others, however, contend that gays as well as non-gays fall on a broad spectrum of health. Some have emotional problems of varying degrees of severity; many are just plain folks who go along living their lives and doing the best they can. It is important to keep in mind that, in some ways, it is "easier" to be drunk/drugged/crazy than it is to be gay in this society. One critically important role of the treatment provider is to offer hope to gay and lesbian alcoholics that they can live their lives in sobriety with dignity and pride.

Our Assumptions About Our Readers

As readers of this book, you may already be involved in or interested in helping alcoholics, such as volunteers, social workers, nurses, doctors, counselors, psychologists, clergy, nurses' aides. We use the word "counselor" as a generic term referring to and addressing all such people.

You, the reader, are a caring, concerned person of good will with basically good attitudes. You tend to be tolerant of diversity and difference and to appreciate the need for acknowledging each individual's worth. In addition, you are willing to work further on your attitudes and are open to change.

You have a working knowledge of alcoholism and are familiar with counseling techniques and how to use them.

You want to understand more about the special issues of gay/lesbian alcoholics in order to be more effective in your counseling of them.

It is possible for you to learn from others' experience; thus our sharing of our knowledge and experience will assist you in becoming more skilled at working with gay/lesbian alcoholics.

Your knowledge of alcoholism probably comes either from hands-on experience or from your own life experience. As a result, you know about the stigmatizing effects of alcoholism — how it pushes people to deny, to isolate, to try to hide or be invisible, to live a double life, to struggle with pain. This experience and knowledge puts you in a rare position of being

11

able to draw on your own experiences and empathize with and really understand gay/lesbian alcoholics and their struggles to recover. In addition, many people who have struggled with other difficult life issues acquire a very special perspective on life and often seem to have a rare strength and balance. To whatever degree you have worked through your own life issues, you have the ability to appreciate the strength, courage, and balance of gay/lesbian alcoholics who have recovered.

Because you care enough to be reading this book, you are indeed special. Welcome!

Arrangement of Information

The book is divided into three major parts. Part I supplies information basic to understanding the issues and problems specific to gay men and lesbians. The section then examines how these issues and problems affect gay men and lesbians who are alcoholics as well as the treatment they receive. In other words, before a gay/lesbian alcoholic even walks through your door, you should know these things.

Part II includes information and skills you will use directly in treatment.

Part III gives information about the resources you will need in order to assist your clients.

The use of several terms needs to be clarified. The words *gay men* and *lesbian* refer respectively to men and women who are homosexual. The term *gay/lesbian* is an adjective denoting both gay men and lesbians. The reason for making these distinctions is that the word *gay* is usually male-identified; thus, a number of women prefer the term *lesbian* as a way of distinguishing themselves as women and their issues as those that are female-identified. However, the only general term (other than the word *homosexual*) is the word "gay." We prefer the term *gay* because the term *homosexual* is heavily male-identified, because it has a cold clinical sound, and because it emphasizes sexuality while excluding the equally important

12

emotional aspects. Thus, we use *gay* as a cover term for gay men and lesbians.

This difficulty with terminology reflects a basic problem in discussing two very different groups of people as though they were the same just because they both belong to a larger grouping. For example, lesbians are more like all women than they are like gay men. Yet for the purposes of this book, we are discussing gay men and lesbians together because they share some similar issues and problems in recovery. This is indeed a general book. More specific and detailed books remain to be written on the specific issues and problems of lesbians and gay men who are alcoholic.

One last comment is in order here. Although you may spend only a short time with each gay/lesbian client and although you may be only a small part in the long process of recovery, whatever kindness, support, and respectful treatment you provide has an impact far beyond the act itself. Your humane treatment in a frequently hostile, oppressive society can tip the balance toward sobriety.

PART ONE

BACKGROUND INFORMATION FOR TREATING GAY/LESBIAN ALCOHOLICS

Facts And Definitions

Because our culture has great difficulty talking, teaching, or learning about any aspect of sexuality, most of us continue to have trouble feeling at ease with the topic. Many of us can kid about sex, tell or laugh at dirty jokes, and can enjoy sexual subjects when "parent figures" are not looking. But a great number of us have difficulty talking openly, seriously, respectfully about sex and sexuality. Because it is already so difficult for some people to discuss sex and sexuality, their resistance increases greatly when the specific topic is homosexuality or any other form of sexuality which differs from the mainstream.

Most people know very little about sexuality in general and homosexuality in particular. Many homosexuals know very little about homosexuality. This lack of knowledge creates feelings of discomfort and generates resistance to discussing or dealing with these subjects. One commonly hears from gay clients in treatment programs and from counselors who work in those programs about the attitudes expressed toward sexuality and homosexuality. For example, some alcoholism treatment units philosophize, "We deal with alcoholism here, not sex; what people do in bed is their business." The rules of many halfway houses state that clients should not have sex for the three or six months they live there, and the halfway houses tend to not deal with problems concerning sex and sexual identity or orientation.

Counselors' Knowledge

For alcoholism counselors to help and support their clients, it is essential to address certain matters. They need to recognize and, if necessary, clarify and perhaps alter their own sexual values and attitudes — certainly their own homophobia. It is important to not just hear what one's "liberal head" says; it's also important to feel what the "gut" does when one interacts with people whose experiences are very different from one's own, such as the man who is effeminate; the woman who is "overly" masculine; the man who cross-dresses; or the woman who feels she is really a man trapped in a woman's body. Counselors also need to explore their own psychosexual functioning and determine what they consider to be the parameters of health. They can ask themselves, is there room in their definition of health for alternative lifestyles? Is being transsexual a healthy way of life? Is homosexuality, like being left-handed, a naturally occurring phenomenon? Is bisexuality a viable orientation? In addition, counselors need to identify areas where they lack education and information and then fill in these gaps. Counselors will then be more comfortable and knowledgeable about sexuality, including homosexuality and other forms of sexual expression.

It is imperative that counselors be as clear as possible about issues regarding sexuality and sexual orientation; clients, whether gay or non-gay, are often confused and frightened about these matters. Many clients were confused about sexual matters before they started drinking or drugging. During their active alcoholism, many of them then engaged in sexual behaviors or experienced emotional attractions which further confused and frightened them. When they start getting sober and struggling with issues related to their sexuality, they are likely to experience a great deal of turmoil. Knowledgeable counselors with nonjudgmental attitudes can help ease the turmoil somewhat and reassure clients it is possible to get sober and come to terms with life in sobriety.

Counselors often see clients who are experiencing such turmoil. Ted, 36, signed himself into an alcoholism unit because he could not stop drinking and was depressed and suicidal. Although he attended A.A. regularly, he kept slipping. When questioned by a counselor whose manner was both accepting and matter-of-fact, he haltingly and painfully shared his past for the first time with anyone. As an adolescent he dressed in women's clothing; even though he stopped doing this after a couple of years he continued to feel very confused and guilty about his behavior. During the past fifteen years, he reported having both hetero- and homosexual experiences, including a four year relationship with a woman he really cared about. In the past few years he struggled to get and stay sober but did not succeed. Although he often went to A.A. meetings, he said he felt alienated and unable to trust others. He did not feel free to talk to anyone about his feelings or experiences. He didn't know where he belonged, who he was, or what he should do. His despair was profound.

Assessing this man's sexual orientation is a difficult and delicate task. But the attempt must be made, along with helping him address his alcoholism, because his sexual orientation issues seem to be affecting his ability to remain sober. An accurate assessment requires the counselor to know a certain amount about transvestism, homosexuality, heterosexuality, and bisexuality. If, for example, a counselor does not know that over 90 percent of transvestites are heterosexual, he or she might conclude this man is probably gay because of his cross-dressing and because of some

17

homosexual experiences. The counselor might, on those bases, urge him to go to gay A.A. meetings. Such conclusions could well be inaccurate, and such urging would be premature and probably very distressing.

If, however, the counselor is relatively well-versed in matters of sexuality and is comfortable discussing them, he or she can help this client explore his sexuality rather than jumping to conclusions or urging actions that may not be appropriate. The first assessment is likely to be that there can be no full assessment until the client had stayed sober for a period of time. Just telling him this may reassure him and help him to relax and give himself time. Also, if there is a knowledgeable therapist in the area, telling this client he can be referred to this person is likely to be reassuring.

It is not the counselor's job to treat the client's sexual identity confusion. What is most important is the counselor attending to the client's statements and feelings; the counselor being empathetic and supportive; and, most of all, the counselor offering some hope for the future if the client can get sober.

A second example will further illuminate the need for information and comprehension. A client at an alcoholism rehabilitation unit had been referred by an agency which gave only a sketchy history. When the counselor took a thorough psychosocial-sexual history, she learned from the client that she had been a "he" and had had transsexual surgery two years before. The counselor was angry at the referring agency for, she felt, misleading the unit about the "man's" sexual identity. That was one issue and was dealt with directly with the referring agency. But the other, less easily resolved issue was the counselor's attitude: she felt she could not accept this transsexual person as a woman. It took much soul-searching, talking to others who had worked with or knew transsexuals, and reading before this counselor finally was able to understand and accept this client. What was important was the counselor could admit her feelings, do something about them, and assign the client to another counselor who was not as emotionally plugged in and could be more helpful.

In order to be somewhat comfortable when trying to assist clients who are in turmoil about sexuality and sexual orientation, it is helpful to be familiar with certain terms and concepts. The discussion that follows is designed to provide some familiarity with these matters. The definitions and explanations are non-technical and are intended only as working definitions and concepts. Sexuality, sexual orientation, and major issues relating to them are extremely complex matters. We urge you to read the materials on the suggested reading lists to broaden and deepen your knowledge and understanding.

Basic Definitions

Certain definitions are basic. *Sex* is used here to refer to biology and anatomy. If a child is born with female sex organs (uterus, ovaries) and female hormones, then she is of the female *sex*. If a child is born with male sex organs (penis, testes) and male hormones, he is of the male *sex*. The concept of *sex*, as used here, refers purely to biological and anatomical make-up; it is separate and distinct from the *feelings* a person (or other people) may have toward his or her biological/anatomical *sex*.

Gender identity refers to psychosocial and cultural factors. It is the sense a person has of him- or herself as a male or female; it concerns the *feelings* a person has about his or her biological/anatomical sex. Gender identity is the way a person sees and expresses him- or herself as a member of the male or female sex; it is the way a person relates to his or her sex.

Closely allied with gender identity is *sex role*. A person's sex role consists of those characteristics, activities, and behaviors which society says are proper for someone of a particular sex. For example, a female in this society is generally socialized to be somewhat non-aggressive, submissive, nurturing; a male is expected to be aggressive, dominating, tough. If sex roles are

19

fairly broad and generous, then people do not have as much problem fitting into them. But if the sex roles tend to be stereotyped (as is true in this culture), then the expectations set up by the roles are rigid, limited, and limiting. They tend to be set forth in far-ranging generalizations which unfortunately wield great power, such as, real men don't cry or ambitious women are not feminine and probably won't get married.

People tend to evaluate themselves and to construct their gender identity according to the strictures of sex role stereotypes, and this often causes confusion and gender identity problems for those who cannot easily match up with the stereotypes. Much of this confusion results from not distinguishing between conformity to sex-role stereotypes and actual feelings toward one's sex. It is important to understand it is often difficult to make a clear-cut distinction between sex role and gender identity. In addition, there is often much confusion about the distinction between gender identity issues and sexual orientation.

For example, suppose a gay man whose manner is rather effeminate is distressed by his mannerisms. He may be quite accepting of his gayness and perfectly clear that he is indeed biologically a male. But he is unhappy because he feels his behavior is unmanly, that it does not match the behavior of a "real man." This is a gender identity problem which is rooted in sex-role stereotypes. Or suppose a non-gay woman who looks quite unlike the feminine stereotypes portrayed by the media has learned to be aggressive, dominating, independent, and tough. She may feel ill at ease and question her femininity and her desirability as a woman even though she is totally clear about being a female. This is more of a sex role stereotype problem which has links to gender identity issues.

Situations and feelings like these can lead to confusion and pain because sex role stereotype and gender identity issues so often get misidentified as sexual orientation issues. For instance, the woman described above may worry about possibly being gay because that is how both she and others interpret her not fitting the sex role stereotype. It is extremely important for counselors to be aware of the differences between gender identity and sexual orientation, so they can accurately assess the information and situations presented by each client and offer appropriate assistance.

Sexual orientation refers to a person's attractions and sexual behavior. Thus the sexual orientation of a *homosexual* involves sexual desire or behavior that is directed toward a person or persons of the same sex. The sexual orientation of a *heterosexual* is directed toward a person or persons of the other sex. The *bisexual* is one whose sexual desire or behavior is directed toward persons of both sexes, though not necessarily at the same time.

Although sexual orientation is ordinarily used to designate a person's sexual behavior, its wider, more comprehensive application involves human relationships and emotions. The term refers not just to what people "do in bed," but to who they are as complete human beings. And because people are complex and are not static, they do not always fit neatly into distinct categories of sexual/affectional orientation. The world is *not* divided into separate camps of 90 percent "pure" heterosexuals and ten percent "pure" homosexuals. Rather, there is a wide range of experience, a broad continuum of sexual/affectional orientation where human beings fit.

In addition, human sexuality is a dynamic condition. Many people shift positions on the continuum of sexual/affectional behavior during the course of their lifetimes. It is extremely important, therefore, to understand that homosexual, heterosexual, and bisexual can be inaccurate or misleading labels because they do not account for the subtleties and intricacies of human emotions and behavior, or for changes in the human condition. For example, what label is correct for a man who is primarily attracted to women but who has had one or two sexual/emotional experiences with men? What is an accurate label for a woman whose primary emotional (and perhaps sexual) interests are in women but who marries and

21

has a family? What of the man who has had many same-sex attractions and experiences and has lived as a gay man for many years, yet he meets a woman and falls in love with her? What of the woman who has been married for many years, gets divorced, and later discovers she is attracted to other women? These examples merely hint at the rich variety of human experiences, perspectives, and emotions. Although labels can be useful, it is crucial to remember they cannot do justice to the complexities of human nature and experience. The labels must, therefore, be applied with great care and be regarded with great caution.

The Kinsey Scale

Alfred Kinsey and his colleagues made invaluable contributions to defining and understanding the enormous range and complexity of human sexual experience.[1] To help describe the meaning of their findings based on over ten thousand interviews with men and women, Kinsey and his colleagues worked out the Kinsey Scale to reflect the continuum of human sexual experience. (See Figure 1.)

Figure 1

```
|-------+-------+-------+-------+-------+-------|
0       1       2       3       4       5       6
```

0. Exclusively heterosexual.
1. Predominantly heterosexual, only incidentally homosexual.
2. Predominantly heterosexual, but more than incidentally homosexual.
3. Equally heterosexual and homosexual.
4. Predominantly homosexual, but more than incidentally heterosexual.
5. Predominantly homosexual, only incidentally heterosexual.
6. Exclusively homosexual.

Kinsey's research revealed that 50 percent of American males were "0's" (exclusively heterosexual) and the remaining 50 percent were spread out along the continuum; these facts refute the belief that the overwhelming majority of society (at least male society) is exclusively heterosexual. Robert T. Francoeur presents Fred Klein's break-out of Kinsey's statistics which gives a clearer picture of the broad range of male sexual/affectional experience.[2]

Figure 2

		Percentage
Kinsey 0 rating	Exclusively other-sex oriented in behavior and psychological response	50
Kinsey 1 rating	Incidental same-sex behavior	15
Kinsey 2 rating	More than incidental same-sex behavior	12
Kinsey 3 rating	About equal amounts of same and other-sex behavior	9
Kinsey 4 rating	More than incidental other-sex behavior	6
Kinsey 5 rating	Incidental other-sex behavior	5
Kinsey 6 rating	Exclusively same-sex oriented in behavior and psychological response	4

"Note: Percentages are rounded off, so that they add up to 101 percent. The breakdown given by Klein (1978) is somewhat confusing because individuals tend to 'float' between categories."[3] This comment by Francoeur underlines the contention that positioning on the continuum of human sexual experience can be fluid.

Other factors revealed by Kinsey's data were equally illuminating. In regard to the period between adolescence and old age, more than one in three men (37 percent) and more than one in eight women (thirteen percent) disclosed that they had had at least one same-sex experience resulting in orgasm. In addition, more recent statistics give evidence that over 30 million Americans have engaged in both heterosexual and homosexual experiences, a phenomenon that suggests some people shift positions on the Kinsey Scale during their lifetimes.[4]

Broadening the Perspectives

Counselors can be most helpful to all their clients if they broaden their perspectives on the dynamic nature of human sexuality and the potential for movement on the continuum of sexual experience. This discussion is not intended to imply everyone changes positions on the continuum; such is certainly not the case. It is intended to point out that not everyone's sexual orientation, attitudes, feelings, behavior, or experience are etched in stone. It can be helpful to clients to hear there is a continuum which allows leeway for differences. The Kinsey Scale can be a helpful tool in assisting a client to begin talking about and looking at his or her sexual orientation. Asking clients to place themselves on the scale may be less threatening than asking them to answer the counselor directly or to use the words gay, lesbian, or homosexual. Often it is easier to say, "I guess I might be a '4'," than to say, "Yes — I am a lesbian (or gay male)."

Klein's way of viewing sexual orientation is broader in scope and more specific.[5] He uses seven interrelated aspects of sexuality. These are:

- **Sexual attraction.** Who turns you on? Who do you find attractive as a real or potential sexual partner?
- **Sexual behavior.** Who are your sexual contacts (partners)?
- **Sexual fantasies.** Who do you enjoy fantasizing about in erotic daydreams?
- **Emotional preference.** With whom do you prefer to establish strong emotional bonds?
- **Social preference.** Which sex do you prefer to spend your leisure time with, and with which sex do you feel most comfortable?
- **Lifestyle.** With whom do you spend most of your daily free time?

• **Self-identification.** How do you identify yourself, in terms of sexual orientation, on the Kinsey Scale?

The answers to these questions are not static; instead, they should be viewed as dynamic in nature, having a past, a present, and a future. In fact, Klein presents a Sexual Orientation Grid which helps people gain a dynamic overview of their sexual orientation.[6] Although Klein uses one to seven for the grid, we use zero to six to match the Kinsey Scale.

Counselors can give their clients the grid in *Figure 3*, (on page 26), with the following instructions. They are to use the 0 to 6 Kinsey numbering that corresponds to the Kinsey Scale numbers as follows:

Zero in any of the 21 boxes indicates that your behavior, attraction, fantasies, emotional or social preference, lifestyle, or self-identification have been, are, or ideally would be exclusively with members of the other sex.

One in any box indicates that your sexual behavior, attraction, fantasies, emotional or social preference, lifestyle, or self-identification have been, are, or ideally would be primarily with members of the other sex but with incidental involvement with persons of your sex.

Two in any box indicates that your sexual behavior, attraction, fantasies, emotional or social preference, lifestyle, or self-identification have been, are, or ideally would involve mostly members of the other sex, but with significant involvement with members of your sex.

Three in any box indicates nearly equal involvement with members of both sexes.

Four in a box indicates involvement mostly with members of the same sex as you, but with significant involvement with members of the other sex.

Five is the reverse of a "one," predominantly same-sex involvement with incidental sex involvement or orientation with the other sex.

Six is exclusive involvement with or orientation toward members of the same sex as you.

In addition, because the Kinsey Scale does not provide for asexual behavior (no sexual behavior, experience, or fantasy), counselors can instruct clients to place a dash (—) wherever appropriate. It is also wise to advise them that the grid's categories are not really distinct and separate and need to be viewed as representing a continuum.

Figure 3

Klein's Sexual Orientation Grid[7]

In order to ascertain your sexual orientation, add the numbers in the 21 boxes and divide by 21 in order to see where you place on the Kinsey Scale. If you have a dash in any box, divide by one less for each dash. You can then ask yourself if this grid is a fairly accurate indicator of your sexual orientation.

	Past	Present (in past year)	Ideal Future Goal
Sexual attraction			
Sexual behavior			
Sexual fantasies			
Emotional preference			
Social preference			
Self-identification			
Lifestyle			

Filling out this grid can help reassure clients by showing them they belong within the range of human sexual behavior. It can also help them begin to examine their sexual and affectional orientation and what that may mean for their lives and their sobriety. And counselors can use the grid to teach clients about the broad range of human sexual, affectional, social, emotional, intellectual, and spiritual experience. They can also use it to underscore the truth that human sexuality and its expressions can change or remain the same over time.

It is also important for counselors to give themselves the experience of filling out the grid. Taking this risk is a positive step on the path to greater openness and ease with the whole topic of sexuality. Such an experience can provide counselors with a vital awareness of their own sexual/affectional orientation and their sexuality. Carrying out such an exercise, evaluating their own sexuality, learning about such instruments as the Kinsey Scale and the Klein Grid, and gaining more information about gay men and lesbians hopefully will have the desired effect — counselors broadening their perception of healthy sexual/affectional orientation to include the whole continuum of human sexuality. By doing so, counselors become much more able to assist their clients in dealing with whatever pain or conflict they may be experiencing as a result of their fears and worries about sexual orientation. That assistance may take many different forms: it may mean getting a client to fill out the grid and talk about its meaning; or helping a client disclose his or her gay or lesbian identity in a group; or providing the client with a safe and accepting "space" where he or she can feel free enough to begin looking more closely at him- or herself.

Transvestism

Transvestism is a complex phenomenon which must be viewed within a cultural context. For example, in most urban and suburban areas in America, women have a good deal of freedom about how they dress. They can wear slacks or dresses; they can wear makeup or no makeup; they can wear boots or high heels — and, for the most part, this goes unnoticed or unremarked. But men in this culture have no such latitude; they are sharply restricted in what they wear. If a man dresses in clothing that borders on being feminine, he risks being labelled a "sissy" or possibly a homosexual. If he wears a dress, uses makeup, or wears high heels, he will very likely be branded a "queer" or a "faggot." Because of these powerful cultural attitudes, transvestism is essentially a *male* phenomenon; a woman would have to go to great extremes of dress in order to be considered a transvestite in Twentieth Century America.

A *transvestite* is a person who compulsively cross-dresses in one or more pieces of clothing ordinarily associated with the opposite sex. Initially, a transvestite cross-dresses because it is sexually arousing to him. Later, this cross-dressing may lose or keep its sexual charge but will usually shift over to or be accompanied by psychological compulsions which are not necessarily erotic in nature. A transvestite cross-dresses to satisfy erotic needs which are in keeping with his particular sexual orientation (e.g., a heterosexual transvestite cross-dresses in order to satisfy his heterosexual erotic needs). It is important to note that although some homosexual males cross-dress, transvestism is predominantly a male heterosexual phenomenon.

It is important to be aware of another phenomenon to understand its relationship to transvestism. Some male homosexuals dress in women's clothing and wear makeup some or much of the time (known as dressing in drag or being a drag queen). They do so for many different reasons — to earn a living as a female impersonator, to express the feminine part of their nature, to rebel, to entertain, to play (known as "camp" or "camping it up"), or to make a political statement. What distinguishes this behavior from transvestism is the intent and psycho-sexual effect on the person who is cross-dressing. If a homosexual male cross-dresses in order to become sexually aroused or if his cross-dressing is compulsive, then that would be considered transvestism. If he cross-dresses for the reasons described above, that is different from transvestism. It is a male homosexual cultural phenomenon.

It is possible, then, that the label of *transvestite* could be inaccurate, misleading, and confusing if applied without a clear understanding of its meaning and without accurate information about the individual being considered. Thus it is extremely important for counselors to learn more about this phenomenon to assist their clients. Rather than being one more representative of society's very restrictive attitudes toward diversity, counselors can reassure their clients by an accepting attitude toward variety and diversity. Counselors can help male clients understand dressing in women's clothing does not necessarily mean that they are gay; nor does it necessarily mean they are not gay. Cross-dressing is simply not an accurate indicator of sexual orientation. Cross-dressing or dressing in drag are not symptoms of mental illness either. It is true that cross-dressing and drag can create problems for people by evoking rejection and ridicule, and they may need the counselor's assistance. But often what is most helpful is the reassurance that transvestism is a far from rare behavior which falls well within the broad range of human sexual behavior.

Transsexual

A *transsexual* is a person whose gender identity conflicts with his or her anatomy. That is, a biological male who believes and feels himself to be a woman in a man's body is a transsexual. A biological woman who believes herself to be a man in a woman's body is a transsexual. The majority of transsexuals are heterosexual. This means, for example, that a biological male who is transsexual with heterosexual feelings is attracted to other men just as a heterosexual woman is attracted to a man. Some transsexuals are homosexual. This means, for example, that a biological male who is transsexual with homosexual feelings is attracted to women just as a

29

lesbian is attracted to other women. The significance of counselors understanding these distinctions is that if a transsexual enters treatment for alcoholism during his or her transition phase, the ways in which this client dresses, behaves, and relates to others are frequently confusing and can be deeply disturbing to other clients and the staff.

Depending on whether or not a transsexual person has had hormone treatments and surgery, he or she will be dealing with different issues and problems. The more information and understanding of transsexuality a treatment center staff has, the easier it will be for them to deal sensitively with the issues. This may involve helping clients and staff with their attitudes, being able to help the transsexual client with his or her drinking rather than focusing primarily on the transsexuality, and openly addressing some of the touchy problems which may arise. These may include such questions as which bathroom this client should use, whether he or she should be on a male or female unit, what sex the roommate should be, whether the client should be referred to as "he" or as "she." To say the least, a creative, flexible, accepting viewpoint and the ability and willingness to hear what the client says and feels will be the most help in this situation.

Two other matters need to be considered in this section: the etiology of homosexuality and the incidence of alcoholism among lesbians and gay men.

Etiology of Homosexuality

Probably the most frequently asked question about homosexuality is, "What causes it?" Indeed, it would be helpful to know what causes homosexuality. It would be equally helpful to know what causes heterosexuality. A number of different "causes of homosexuality" have been posited; genetic factors, hormonal imbalances, arrested psychosexual development, and societal/familial conditioning are major ones. But the truth of the matter is, no one really knows. Perhaps the best and most accurate way to view the etiology of homosexuality is through a metaphor. Homosexuality, like left-handedness, is a phenomenon naturally occurring in a certain percentage of the population. This view is supported by Clellan S. Ford's and Frank A. Beach's findings that 64 percent of societies they studied considered homosexual behavior as acceptable in certain individuals.[8] Kinsey, his colleagues, and others pointed out that homosexuality occurs in almost every mammalian species.[9] If everyone subscribed to the view that homosexuality is a naturally occurring phenomenon, life would be much better for gay men and lesbians — as well as for heterosexuals.

Incidence of Alcoholism

The incidence of alcoholism among lesbians and gay men is often a sharply debated question. Despite a lack of accurate and detailed data, the few research efforts that have been done support one another's findings and suggest alcoholism and/or alcohol abuse currently affect about one-third of American gay men and lesbians. M. T. Saghir and his associates stated 30 percent of the gay men and 35 percent of the lesbians studied were dependent on alcohol or drank excessively.[10] Martin S. Weinberg and Colin J. Williams found 29.4 percent of the male homosexual population they studied reported "drinking more than they should," that is, drinking nearly "all the time."[11] Lillene Fifield and her associates reported, "Fully one-third of the total gay population in Los Angeles County abuse alcohol on a regular basis, and . . . alcohol abuse has been built into the social fabric of this minority lifestyle."[12] L. Lohrenz and his associates examined alcohol problems among gay males in four midwestern cities.[13] Their study revealed that 29 percent of the 145 respondents were categorized as alcoholic on the basis of their Michigan Alcoholism Screening Test (MAST) scores. Roger Beatty reported on the findings of two gay counseling centers in Pennsylvania.[14] Both centers discovered 40 percent of their new admissions had MAST scores indicative of alcoholism.

With such a high incidence rate, one might assume alcohol treatment centers would have many gay/lesbian patients. Yet one study done on this subject reported that of 54,000 clients treated for alcoholism in Los Angeles County over a six-month period, only one percent was identified as gay.[15] But, of the 46 agencies surveyed, the twenty claiming to have any gay clients made this determination on the basis of staff judgments concerning client dress and personal mannerisms!

With such a high incidence rate, one might hope, if not assume, that the gay and lesbian communities would be alarmed and would mobilize to fight against this terrible threat. Although some groups such as NALGAP have done so, unfortunately, in a number of the subcultures (other than the recovering A.A., Al-Anon, ACOA, other addictions, and health-focused groups) quite the opposite is the case. *Alcophobia,* the irrational fear and dread of information about alcoholism and chemical dependency, permeates these subcultures. The prevailing philosophy often seems to be living the gay or lesbian life inevitably involves drinking and getting high.

External Homophobia

There are a number of issues and problems that are specific to gay/lesbian alcoholics' experience and that can increase the difficulty of their recovery from alcoholism and other drug dependencies. The central issue, from which all the others seem to arise, is *homophobia* — an intense, irrational fear and dread of homosexuality and homosexuals. Since George Weinberg coined the word in 1972, its meanings and connotations have broadened, so it generally now refers to all prejudicial attitudes or feelings toward homosexuals.[16] Homophobia includes the irrational fear and dread of as well as the hatred and contempt for homosexuality and all gay men and lesbians. Homophobia permeates American culture like the air we breathe; thus, it is virtually impossible for any of us to grow up without becoming homophobic. Everyone — both gay and non-gay — seems to be homophobic to some degree.

Homophobia is comprised of all the unfounded and prejudicial teachings and beliefs about homosexuality held to be true by the culture and perpetuated by society's various institutions. These negative attitudes affect both gays and non-gays. Non-gay women who walk down the street hand in hand or even arm in arm run the risk of being branded as lesbians; and if non-gay men were to do so, they would most likely be ridiculed as "faggots" or "fairies." Thus homophobia seriously restricts the freedom and spontaneity of both gay and non-gay people. In addition, Weinberg contends that homophobia affects mental health.[17] If people, whether gay or not, are homophobic, their choices of responding to others and to life are limited and compromised. Society's negative attitudes are, however, incalculably more powerful and destructive for gay men and lesbians. An appreciation of these effects can help counselors begin to understand why their gay/lesbian clients might be frightened to reveal their sexual orientation, might be extremely mistrustful, or might have special issues affecting their recovery from alcoholism.

Religion

Citing from Scripture and dogma, many religious institutions have led the attack against homosexuality, branding it sinful, immoral, and against the laws of God and Nature. Although in recent years some churches have taken a more liberal view, many continue to condemn homosexuality as an affront to God and a danger to the heart of Judeo-Christian life — marriage and the family. The gay male or lesbian client who seeks help for alcoholism is well aware of religious homophobia. It appears in newspaper columns written by fundamentalist preachers who sometimes equate homosexuality with the "Communist threat," and a few who call for the literal extermination of homosexuals. It appears in the Pope's statement that acting upon one's homosexual feelings is a sin. It appears in people's comments that AIDS victims are only getting what they deserve, that God is punishing them for their sins.

Religious homophobia does not confine its destructive effects to homosexuality. A number of fundamentalists equate homosexuality with alcoholism and view both as self-induced, self-inflicted moral sicknesses. Their contention is that all homosexuals and alcoholics have to do is repent, pray, and give up their sinful condition. Perhaps they cannot help becoming alcoholic or homosexual, but they can give it up! Such attitudes tend to evoke rage — and if not rage, then despair.

The client sitting in front of the counselor may have stopped going to church long ago because of the tremendous guilt instilled by his or her religion. A number of gays report the traumatic results of confessing their homosexual behavior or perhaps just their feelings to priests and having the priests castigate them or refuse absolution. Many gays describe their despair as they measured their feelings and behavior against their churches' teachings and learned that by those standards they were sinners. Because of these kinds of conflicts and emotional scars, many gay people may have extra trouble in sobriety with spiritual concepts involving "moral" inventories and mentioning a belief in God. Fortunately, nuns, priests, ministers, or rabbis can often help heal some of the scars simply by acting in an accepting and understanding manner.

The Medical/Psychiatric Profession

Late in the Nineteenth Century, the medical/psychiatric profession somewhat tempered the prevailing religious view of homosexuality by defining it as a mental aberration, a form of illness, and claiming it should be treated, not condemned as sinful. Since that time, much homophobia has simply taken on a pseudo-scientific aura, and many gay men and lesbians have been subjected to all kinds of indignities, insults, and poor treatment by health professionals under the guise of therapy or treatment. A number of lesbians have reported their gynecologists have told them to have intercourse to "get over" or "outgrow" their lesbianism. Gay men have been subjected to electric shocks in aversive therapy to condition them to not respond erotically to other men. And there are reports of lobotomies and other brain surgeries being performed on gay men and lesbians in attempts to "cure" them of their homosexuality.[18]

Up until 1973, the American Psychiatric Association (APA) labelled homosexuality as an illness and so listed it in the *Diagnostic and Statistical Manual of Mental Disorders*.[19] After careful consideration as well as much discussion and disagreement, the APA declared homosexuality "by itself does not necessarily constitute a psychiatric disorder." It goes on to say that only if a person is unable to accept and adjust to being homosexual can he or she be considered as sick, a state labelled "Ego-Dystonic Homosexuality." Categorizing the inability to accept homosexuality as pathological seems rather inappropriate given the high level of homophobia in this culture. In addition, officially getting rid of labels does not automatically get rid of homophobic attitudes.

In spite of the APA's declaration, many psychologists and psychiatrists continue to view homosexuality as mental illness; it is not unusual to hear of gays being treated as though the essence of their emotional problems — if such are present — is their "abnormal" lifestyles. Many gays still report having psychiatrists, psychologists, and other professionals urge them to change their sexual orientation or offer to "cure" them. Countless gay men and lesbians have been subjected to hostile and destructive treatment based on the psychological views that gays are the way they are because of "arrested psychosexual development" or because of neuroses. This latter, unfortunately common situation is analogous to the view that alcoholism is a symptom of an underlying personality disorder. Urging a lesbian or gay man to gain insight, change her or his behavior, and thereby be "cured of homosexuality" is much like exhorting an alcoholic to do the same with her or his alcoholism. Both sets of exhortations are rooted in ignorance, prejudice, fear, and hostility.

Just as destructive are the more subtle instances when counselors simply ignore the issue of homosexuality. Because of ignorance and homophobia, they are in denial and do not attend to the realities of the person in front of them by asking and actively seeking to know the person's background, experiences, and feelings about sexual identity. This is similar to many psychiatrists, psychologists, and doctors who fail to ask clients about their alcohol use — because of the helping professionals' prejudices and resultant denial. Obviously, it is difficult if not impossible to give proper service when blinded by prejudice.

The Legal System

It is possible gay/lesbian clients may be filled with terror at being discovered, either because they have already been caught in the legal system or because they are frightened by the threat of legal action against them. Many gays have been in a gay bar when a police raid swept through. Other gays have been roughed up or arrested by the police on flimsy charges. And most gays live daily with the knowledge and fear that, if discovered, they could lose their jobs, their homes, or their children via custody battles because the law in most cities and states does not afford gays the same protection it affords to non-gay people. In 24 states, it is still a crime punishable by imprisonment for consenting adults of the same sex to have sexual relations with one another.[20] Unfortunately, the states' rights to make and enforce such laws received strong support from the June 1986 Supreme Court ruling which upheld the "Sodomy Law" in Georgia. Even death does not end the discrimination. There are no laws to protect surviving gays when lovers die intestate. Even when there is a will, relatives frequently step in, deny the existence or validity of the lovers' relationship, and claim and receive the inheritance. Thus, even if the gay person needs help from a counselor, he or she may be determined to not reveal who he or she really is. Fear of the law and how people may use it is extremely powerful.

The Media

The media reinforces the message to gays that self-revelation invites ridicule or pity, if not rage and contempt. The intensity of homophobia in the media ranges from the subtle negative messages sent by omission (portrayals of ordinary, everyday gay/lesbian people are notably lacking on TV and in movies, magazines, and newspapers) to reporting that sensationalizes homosexuality and homosexuals. We have only to remember how the media focused on and squeezed every drop of "scandal" out of Rock Hudson's life and death. Furthermore, crimes committed by people labelled as homosexual are avidly reported as especially terrible, whereas child molestation by a heterosexual male does not usually carry the same emotional charge. Such reporting is a distortion but usually goes unchallenged because of homophobia.

One of today's worst slurs that can be made about a person is that of "homosexual." Ironically, liberal political candidates who are not even supporters of gay rights have been injured by suggestions that they "support and condone homosexuality." Implying that people are "soft" on homosexuality implies they are anti-family, anti-American, and anti-God.

Some current radio talk show hosts regularly make vicious homophobic remarks. And when movies and TV portray gay men or lesbians, they are often shown either as silly or tragic figures. Or the homosexuality is denied or made invisible. Frequently, gay characters in novels and plays are neutralized by being made nongay and nonsexual when a television adaptation is produced. This is a chilling example of the media's power; if the media says something does not exist or does not classify as an acceptable lifestyle, then it does not.

In addition to hearing all the media's negative messages, most gay people are subjected to homophobic remarks every day because most gays pass as heterosexual most of the time. These rather ordinary, invisible gays must hear all the slurs and jokes that people feel free to utter — especially because there seem to be no gays around. They hear the derogatory language casually used to describe gays — faggots, fruits, fairies, dykes, lezzies, butches, femmes, pansies, sissies, and girls. The contempt, fear, and hatred conveyed by these words are a part of the pulse of American life.

Living in the midst of homophobia is one of the more stressful experiences a person can be subjected to. It requires an almost constant struggle to answer such questions as, "Where do I belong?" "Who am I?" "Who will accept me?" "What value do I have?" And the price of openness may be as high as loss of jobs and rejection by the family — the two institutions most directly involved with developing and maintaining identity, self-esteem, and a sense of belonging. Obviously, the stress created by the pressures of homophobia is extremely strong.

When counselors can get in touch with the power of this constant assault on gay/lesbian sensibilities and lives, they can become a positive, counteractive force in the client's recovery. When counselors recognize that most of the world does not have accepting views of homosexuals and, indeed, despises and abuses homosexuals, they are much more able to help. An awareness of the impact of homophobia makes it possible for counselors to empathetically understand why their gay male or lesbian clients may have tried or are honestly claiming to be heterosexual, why they may feel almost unbearable guilt, and why they may be filled with rage, denial, or self-pity. By understanding the implications of life in a homophobic society, counselors are enabled to have a powerful, positive impact on clients' lives. As people who really do understand and care, as people who are accepting and consciously nonhomophobic, counselors can help provide a safe environment for gay/lesbian patients, an experience which offers them that most powerful of all emotions — hope.

Internalized Homophobia

Having to contend with the ever-present pressures of external homophobia on a day-to-day basis is, at best, demanding and disheartening. Dealing with *internalized homophobia* is more difficult and painful. As they grow up, most lesbians and gay men are taught the homophobic values of the culture. Gradually, they *internalize* these values — learn them, accept them as truth, and incorporate them into their belief system. After the lesbians and gay men realize they are homosexual, they apply these values to themselves because they are members of the stigmatized group. Many gays report growing up feeling uneasy about themselves, not sure what was "wrong," but sure "something" was indeed "wrong." As they began to sense or discovered how they were different, many were horrified to learn they belonged to a group reviled by this culture. The feelings generated by internalized homophobia are extremely painful. They are the feelings of a self divided. Many gay people feel the very center of their being is tainted and unacceptable. That which defines who they are becomes the enemy. Now they are beset by two hostile forces — from without and within.

Basic Reactions and Consequences

The consequences of homophobia are often harsh and far-reaching. Some gays react by becoming angry or rebellious, or by acting in ways dangerous to themselves. Some try to, or actually do, commit suicide. Many, perhaps the majority, live and measure their lives according to society's homophobic values, living as if those values were facts and truths. Thus it is not unusual for gays to believe that heterosexuals are superior, homosexuals inferior. Some gays, for instance, do not want a gay counselor for this reason. A number of gays make an "accommodation" with what they see as this "unnatural" part of themselves by grimly living as heterosexuals — because to live openly as gay men or lesbians would mean to them accepting themselves as lesser beings, immoral, stigmatized, and unwanted. Of these, a number will seek what they perceive as the safety of an asexual life in a religious order. Others seem to unconsciously seek a very homophobic setting such as the armed forces. A number of gay men and lesbians we have met spoke of going into the religious life or into military service as a way of "solving" their sexual/affectional conflicts. Some felt these institutions would discipline them and keep their unruly and unacceptable feelings in check. Others felt by sacrificing and serving others they could "save" themselves from their "baser instincts." Unfortunately, such measures tend to increase feelings of self-loathing and blame. And, all too frequently, these people turned to drinking and/or drugging as a seemingly acceptable way to decrease and soothe their psychic pain.

Some lesbians and gay men split their lives and have homosexual experiences and relationships while in heterosexual relationships. Sometimes, in order to deal with the enormous stress generated by their internalized homophobia, gays come to see themselves as "not gay." They may engage in homosexual behavior, but in their minds they are completely identified with heterosexuality. Such is the power of denial in the face of life — or sanity — threatening circumstances. One problem with this behavior, however, is the person often becomes isolated from others and from him- or herself; the person may turn to alcohol and other drugs as a way of coping with the pain of isolation. And, as is well-known, using alcohol and other drugs to cope puts people at risk of becoming chemically dependent.

Depression

Other effects of internalized homophobia are equally harmful. Many gays are filled with self-hatred, self-loathing, and self-contempt — all of which can lead to depression. These feelings can, in turn, contribute to heavy drinking and alcoholism, other drug use, and suicidal thoughts or actions.

Gay men and lesbians who are at risk for chemical dependency may drink or use other drugs to medicate their depression, to fill the void, to kill the pain, or to create the illusion of not being different. But they have no idea that, all the while, the use of chemicals is depressing them further. Thus the depression created by the physiological and psychological effects of being chemically dependent is, for gay people, often heightened and intensified by depression resulting from internalized homophobia.

This phenomenon also creates potential dangers for gay/lesbian alcoholics trying to recover. The depression resulting from internalized homophobia will not necessarily or usually be removed with the removal of alcohol. In fact, it may deepen and place these clients at great risk of relapse. It is important, therefore, that counselors help their gay/lesbian clients begin to find constructive and practical ways to deal with their depression (and thus their homophobia). It is also important to point out to clients that their depression is an appropriate response to the loss of their "best friend, alcohol" which shielded them from the assaults of homophobia. It is also an appropriate response to the homophobia that is all around us and says gay men and lesbians are worthless and contemptible.

Anxiety

In addition to self-hatred and depression, many gays experience powerful, sometimes crippling anxiety. Anxiety may be defined as the way an organism responds to what it perceives as dangerous and threatening. Since this society perceives homosexuality and homosexuals as a frightening threat to its values, it is little wonder that many gays view discovery of their gayness as a great danger and therefore experience anxiety. Because of their internalized homophobia which says the very center of their being is sick and disgusting, it is no wonder so many gay people feel their sexual/affectional orientation must be hidden at all costs. The overriding fear generated by these feelings is of discovery by others and/or by

41

self. "I could not bear it if I were gay." "I would hate myself if I were a lesbian." "I could not live with myself if I found out I was gay." "What would they think of me if they found out?" "If they only knew, they wouldn't like me."

It is not uncommon for gay people to go to some lengths to hide their homosexuality from others, even to the point of fabricating detailed cover stories. For example, many lesbians and gay men will get friends of the opposite sex to go to family functions with them as boy/girlfriends or fiances/fiancees, so family and friends will not know or suspect. Another instance involves the young woman who works on an otherwise all-male construction gang. In order to contend with and defuse the vicious homophobia and sexism she was subjected to, she created a boyfriend, Hank, who she described, showed pictures of, and talked about at great length. Such hiding is commonplace in response to homophobia, both external and internalized.

Coming to terms with internalized homophobia and learning how to cope with external homophobia is a long, complex, painful, and arduous process. It is made so by many gay people's deep, underlying fear that at their very core they are irreparably defective and forever unacceptable to society, to their families and to themselves. With this comes the belief that no matter how well they may do in other aspects of their lives, no matter how brilliant or famous or accomplished they may become — underneath they are no good. Thus, many of them live their lives in fear — that somehow, some way, some day, someone will discover their secret.

Living with such fears, whether they be conscious or not, tends to make some gay people feel very paranoid and they may become hypervigilant, always on the lookout for possible danger. The anxiety produced by living with such fears takes its toll. One way that many gay people learn to deal with the stress of such anxiety is to medicate themselves with alcohol and/or other drugs, a strategy which can all too easily boomerang into dependency. Then they are likely to be afflicted with the agitation, unknown fears, and paranoia common to alcoholism — feelings which heighten and intensify already existing anxiety.

As is true of depression, abstinence usually does not remove the anxiety produced by internalized homophobia. In fact, it may make matters worse. Without anesthesia, gay/lesbian alcoholics' awareness of their anxiety may be much sharper and far less tolerable. Thus they may be at greater risk of relapse. It is important, therefore, that counselors help gay/lesbian clients learn constructive ways to reduce anxiety and assist them to explore the ways homophobia generates anxiety. It is helpful for counselors to acknowledge the powerful, anxiety-producing effects of homophobia because that validates their clients' feelings and aids their reality testing. In addition, such counselor responses are very supportive to frightened clients. The importance of addressing and helping with gay/lesbian clients' anxiety cannot be overstressed. At best, unresolved anxiety is likely to make these clients' sobriety less fulfilling or comfortable than it otherwise might be. At worst, it can lead to relapse.

Defenses

The two major consequences of homophobia, depression and anxiety, are not only destructive but also extremely painful. It is important, therefore, to understand the ways that gay people defend against the homophobia which creates such discomfort. Counselors need to understand what defensive postures they are seeing in their clients in order to know how to react and how to deal with them.

Everyone has defenses. They help us survive. They are the ways our minds have of protecting us from what we perceive as threats or danger; they protect the ways we see and feel about ourselves from devaluation. Defenses are usually considered to be unconscious psychological mechanisms employed to shield the "self" from pain and perceived danger. There are many different defenses, and usually more than one will be in operation at one time.

Defenses are, of course, familiar to anyone who knows about alcoholism, denial being perhaps the most familiar. What is important is that counselors know how to discriminate among the differing reasons gay/lesbian alcoholics may have for utilizing various defenses at different times. Are these defenses being employed to protect the alcoholism or to ward off the assaults of homophobia — or both? These are delicate questions and require a certain amount of knowledge and skill to deal with them constructively. But they need to be attended to and answered.

Since everyone raised in this culture is taught "it's not all right to be gay," it follows that anyone who has a sense, or even faintly suspects, that he or she might be gay or have tendencies "that way" will develop defenses against the danger perceived as inherent in homosexuality. Thus people who have even the slightest inkling they might be "different" (though many are not even sure in what way) will establish ways to protect themselves against knowing or at least against others knowing. Thus many gay men and lesbians have highly developed defensive systems long before they start to drink or use other drugs. Drinking and using other drugs are also defensive postures which are employed by many lesbians and gay men as ways of not knowing, not feeling, or not caring. If they then get addicted, their already established defenses interlock with those generated by their alcoholism — a phenomenon which creates extra strong defenses that can all too effectively get in the way of gay/lesbian alcoholics' treatment and recovery.

While this powerful defense system can make treatment difficult, it is often something counselors can readily understand because of their experience with the alcoholic defense system. It is important that counselors draw on, yet go beyond, this understanding in order to make distinctions that are critical to the treatment process. They need to be aware of the even greater power of gay/lesbian alcoholics' defenses. They need to distinguish between confronting the tough yet brittle defenses that protect alcoholism and respecting those defenses that actually help gays survive against homophobia.

Yet, such matters are not always clear-cut. Frequently what the counselor will do depends on delicate judgments. Being able to evaluate accurately and to make these judgments skillfully depends on counselors having a good grasp of the major defenses that gay men and lesbians use in order to maintain their stability. In addition, counselors will need to do a lot of self-monitoring of their own feelings and reactions to prevent themselves from colluding (and/or colliding) with the clients' defenses. If counselors are in denial of their own homophobia, they may respond to clients who fearfully relate having same-sex experiences while drinking by strongly reassuring clients that they are not gay. Or when confronted by a client who is filled with rage at an unjust homophobic society, a counselor may interpret the behavior generated by that rage as a "poor attitude toward treatment" and unconsciously or semi-consciously "write the patient off" or consider a "therapeutic discharge." Or if clients do not want to disclose their sexual orientation to other clients on a unit, counselors may collude by too readily agreeing to the clients' views and thereby joining the conspiracy of silence; counselors may collide by insisting clients "come out" on the unit when to do so is too threatening.

Obviously, it is extremely important for counselors to know about and understand the major defenses gay men and lesbians use in order to deal with the external and internalized homophobia which constantly confronts them. The five primary defenses are denial, rationalization, reaction formation, hostility and anger, and "passing."

Denial

Probably the most powerful defense of all is denial — a process by which a person unconsciously changes reality so that it suits his or her needs. In denial, people unknowingly create a subjective reality, a world of their own, by reversing or significantly changing the facts of objective reality. In this manner, people are able to prevent themselves from knowing about something which, if they did know about it, would threaten their self-concept and create unbearable anxiety. This defense produces a strange phenomenon: a person can behave in a way which is obvious to others, but he or she is unable to see this behavior. The ways alcoholics employ denial are understood in the alcoholism field as is the primal power of this defense.

The objective reality in a homophobic culture is that it can be dangerous to be gay; the dangers range from insults to bodily harm. For many people, even contemplating the slightest possibility of having any "gay feelings," much less the possibility of being gay, is so dangerous that they unconsciously shut down their perceptions and literally do "not know" they are gay or might have gay feelings. Thus, it is entirely possible and not so uncommon for a person to engage, or to have engaged, in homosexual behavior and not see that behavior as being gay. Or people may be asexual or celibate and not know they have homosexual feelings. Or people may live as heterosexuals and respond unconsciously with denial whenever anything occurs that even whispers of difference.

It is also important to remember that our culture encourages people to deny homosexuality. And the culture itself denies the existence of homosexuality whenever possible. It demands and rewards invisibility, tolerating gay people as long as they remain quiet, docile, and hidden in their closets. The gay person's most total form of invisibility is denial, both to others and to him- or herself. But this defense exacts a high price of unconscious inner stress. It is maintained only by expending enormous amounts of psychic energy. Because this culture sanctions the use of alcohol as a means of relaxing, it is not unusual that people in denial about their sexuality might use alcohol to help them avoid the truth.

46

If the use of alcohol develops into problem drinking and alcoholism, the denial system becomes enormously powerful as the denial of addiction swirls together with the denial of sexuality. The significance of this phenomenon is that removal of the drug may throw people into crisis because they are left with weakened defensive systems; they have to deal with the stresses of raw, newly sober selves.

Basically, people who deny their sexual orientation will unconsciously build their denial and continue in this way. But there may be moments of crisis when the defensive system does not work well enough and people panic. Counselors can be extremely helpful at such junctures by reassuring, accepting, and supporting clients. It is possible and desirable to plant seeds of acceptance which may take root and blossom at a much later time. For example, counselors may reassure clients that fears and confusion about sexual orientation commonly occur in early sobriety, and it is often wise to put such considerations on the shelf. Counselors can also indicate that whatever clients eventually determine about their sexual orientation will be okay. Counselors may give clients books to read about sexuality or may simply assure clients that they can come and talk about their feelings without fear of judgment. Regardless of a counselor's specific actions, it is most important that he or she shows a caring and accepting attitude which clients can "borrow" until they develop their own acceptance.

Reaction Formation

Another very powerful defense is that of reaction formation: people react to what they fear they are or may be by identifying with, acting like, or becoming the opposite. It is not uncommon for people who are motivated in this way to identify with and become like the aggressors who attack the feared group (or characteristic). Thus a person who fears he or she might be homosexual might join a religious group which is especially vocal in its opposition to gays and become an outspoken opponent of all gays. Or this person might just simply be among those who laugh the loudest at anti-gay jokes. By these means, people who fear they might be gay protect themselves against "knowing" or "owning" their potential gayness or against being identified with this hated group. Through this defense, they try to counteract the devaluation of their self-concept.

Knowing about this particular defense will help counselors when confronted by the stereotypical behavior of ultra non-gay people. People who join anti-gay campaigns or who tell offensive jokes do seem, on the face of it, to be gay-hating heterosexuals. But that may be a protective device that hides gays from themselves or others and that channels their self-hatred outward. By recognizing how this defense works, counselors can listen to clients who bad-mouth gays or belong to anti-gay organizations with a better perspective. Such clients may be heterosexual, but destructively homophobic; they may be gay (or terrified of becoming gay) and unable to deal with it. If counselors confront the homophobia, they may help a non-gay client begin to look at attitudes which might hinder serene sobriety, or they may help a gay or lesbian client feel a little more at ease. By addressing the homophobia, counselors will assist people with their sexual identity issues. Counselors can convey a sense of safety and acceptance to clients who are struggling to find a place for themselves in the world.

Rationalization

This defense is especially familiar to those who work with alcoholics. It is the process by which people explain away an event, behavior, thought, or feeling they cannot bear to become aware of. By their explanation, they make it "not so" or at least different from reality. People tend to rationalize when faced with the discovery that they are unacceptable (e.g., homosexual). Rather than suffer a devalued self-concept, they change reality. These rationalizations include unconscious ideas like, "I only did those things because I was drunk"; "I'm really bisexual"; "That's not like me. It's not my fault — I was seduced." "I only did it because I was curious. I'm a free spirit, willing to experience everything." "It was just a phase." Such perceptions make reality less threatening.

Rationalizing results in further turmoil for those who are already confused about their sexual identity. Eventually they may not even know what is real. If problem drinking or alcoholism become part of this muddle, more confusion is created as people begin rationalizing about their drinking. Thus alcohol helps maintain — and in fact intensifies — people's mind-tricks and illusions.

When alcohol is removed, people who are confused about their sexual identity become extraordinarily vulnerable, and their stress levels increase greatly. They need gentle care. Alcoholism has made their nerves raw, and removing the sedative exposes these nerves to the cold air of reality. Abstinence has taken away part of the shield that helped protect them from facing their sexual identity issues. This is not a good time to confront clients' rationalizations about possible gayness; rather, counselors need to be aware of this state and approach these clients with care, restraint, and support. The counselor needs to convey the assurance that sexual identity is something that takes time to work out, that the client is safe with the counselor, and that the client is free to proceed at his or her own pace.

Hostility and Anger

Another defensive reaction is that of acting in hostile and angry ways. Being enraged at injustice is certainly a healthier reaction to homophobia than falling into despair. But when the defense hardens into an automatic, uncontrolled response that keeps others away, it creates problems with intimacy, honesty, and trust. Rage is a dragon guarding the self. If anyone approaches too close by asking questions, or by showing concern, the dragon may rise up in wrath to drive off the intruder.

It is especially important for counselors to recognize the possibility of this defense because it often appears during treatment. For example, gay/lesbian clients may lash out at others with hostile and sarcastic comments, may be argumentative, may angrily withdraw from others, or may challenge everyone and everything. Counselors should be prepared for clients who act out in ultra stereotypical ways: males who "swish about with limp wrists," females who may "stomp around in engineer boots." Clients who are behaving in these ways are difficult to handle. What may be particularly upsetting to counselors is that this kind of rage reaction may be evoked by kindness. Out of concern, a counselor may question the patient with great sensitivity and thereby discover the patient's sexual orientation. The client may become hostile and challenge the counselor's right to ask such personal questions. He or she may be mistrustful and suspicious, and accuse the counselor of hostile motives.

It is helpful to understand and keep in mind the painful sources of such rage and hostility. Thus, counselors can be better prepared to deal calmly and firmly with this defensive reaction and not take the matter personally. By meeting such outpourings of rage, suspicion, mistrust, and hostility with a certain therapeutic balance, counselors can help their clients gain some control over their anger. By not reacting negatively to the patient's "I'll reject you before you reject me" stance, counselors can often disarm the fury and help clients begin to get past their defensive anger and deal with the terrible pain underneath it.

Counselors might say to these clients, "I realize that you're extremely angry. Apparently you feel safe enough here to allow your anger to show. And that's important. But you also must recognize that there are certain rules which must be followed here — not verbally assaulting others; not acting in sexually provocative ways; not deliberately provoking others' anger. In light of these rules, what do you think the way you have been acting means? What kind of messages do you think your behavior sends to others? Perhaps you can work on expressing your anger more directly — either to staff, other patients, or both. It is important, though, that you respect other people's boundaries, that you not pour out your anger onto other people. If you start feeling overwhelmed by your rage, talk to someone — don't act on it. It's a lot like learning not to take a drink. Instead of acting on your impulse to take a drink, you talk to someone." The counselors' specific words may vary, but what is most important is the counselors' acceptance of the person and his or her pain and the counselors' firm refusal to accept abusive and self-destructive behavior.

Passing as Heterosexuals

Many gay men and lesbians present themselves to the world as heterosexuals; they assume a mask or facade of heterosexuality to make their homosexuality invisible. As heterosexuals, it is especially important for counselors to understand this defense because it is a primary and often necessary one used by gay men and lesbians against the assaults of homophobia. While this is mainly a conscious defense, controlled by choice, it helps to know people may use it so often they're not conscious of doing it. Three basic factors relate to the creation of this defense:

- Homosexuality is for the most part a hidden stigmatized condition.
- Society encourages and demands invisibility.
- The danger perceived in revealing a homosexual identity is often very real. In response to these factors, gay men and lesbians learn to defend themselves by passing as heterosexual.

In light of the realities of homophobia, passing is a valid, healthy, adaptive defense required to protect such things as one's safety, self-esteem, job, or family. What is *not* healthy about passing is that it is forced upon gay men and lesbians by society's homophobia and that having to defend oneself against real attacks makes the stakes of self-disclosure very high. In addition, like any other defense, if passing becomes rigid, inflexible, and automatic, then it can be destructive. Some gay people cannot seem to drop the mask and be who they really are even around other gay people. Some gays hide their sexual/affectional identity all their lives, never telling even their closest friends. And some, even when it is clear there would be minimal repercussions, cannot free themselves from their rigid defense to share their identity with others.

There are many ways of passing, from the subtle to the obvious. These tactics include taking an opposite-sex friend to family functions, referring to lovers only by the pronoun "they," and never talking about one's personal life. Many gays force themselves into heterosexual dating patterns in their adolescence and early adulthood. A number of them enter heterosexual marriages and then either have extramarital homosexual affairs or do not acknowledge or act on their homosexual orientation and feelings. The most common form of passing is dressing, talking, and acting as much as possible like a "straight" person whenever interacting with the straight world. The majority of gay men and lesbians in our society pass as straight most of the time and take off their masks only when they feel safe with lovers, friends, or even strangers. For a number of gays, this seems to be a relatively comfortable way of living; many gays have developed tough egos in the course of their fight against homophobia.

Having a tough ego, however, does not completely protect a person from the high price of leading a double life. Creating and maintaining a believable mask requires much energy, skill, vigilance, and a certain sacrifice of self. To live as two people can engender great stress. For some gays, this stress becomes too great and causes serious problems. This split between inner and outer self, occurring over a long period of time, can gradually create strong feelings of confusion, fragmentation, disjunction, and emptiness. It is difficult to retain a clear sense of self and self-worth when one must always hide or deny one's true inner self. Unfortunately, many gay men and lesbians try to mend the split and sedate the pain with alcohol and other drugs. These may be very helpful in assuaging the pain and filling up the empty places — for awhile. But if alcoholism develops, then the addicted person experiences even more feelings of confusion, fragmentation, and emptiness since these are also responses to the disease process of addiction. When this occurs, the gay man's and lesbian's responses to the disease of alcoholism and to the assaults of homophobia intermingle and intensify each other.

The tendency of alcoholics to pass as social drinkers is well-known, as is their tendency to develop masks to hide their drinking, even from themselves. When alcoholics stop drinking and drugging, the terrifying split between their frightened, vulnerable, true inner selves and their falsely brave outer selves often haunts their early recovery. When gay/lesbian alcoholics stop drinking or drugging, they face not only the terror of the splits created by their addiction, but also the agonizing reality of the gulf between their mask of heterosexuality and their true inner selves.

In order to get help with their alcoholism and be able to come to terms with it, alcoholics must stop passing as social drinkers, drop their social drinker mask, and start dealing with their new identity of alcoholic. To assume — by some tenuous analogy — that alcoholics who are gay men or lesbians must also *necessarily* stop passing as heterosexuals, drop their heterosexual mask, and start dealing with their gay/lesbian identity through self-disclosure is a mistake. To assume that unless they do so, these gay/lesbian alcoholics will somehow not recover properly (if at all) is an even greater mistake. For most of them, the process of coming out, of disclosing self, is a long one which should not be forced or rushed.

It is especially important to respect this slowness of pace in the early stages of recovery. To pressure or force gay/lesbian alcoholics to drop their straight masks while they are also required to drop their masks of social drinking is often more than they can manage. That many gay/lesbian alcoholics survive and recover in the face of such demands is a testament to their toughness of spirit. Others never enter treatment or else flee from it and often relapse. Some find help; some do not survive.

The role of counselors in the early recovery of gay/lesbian alcoholics is a very important and sometimes rather delicate one. Oftentimes, counselors may need to serve as buffers between their clients and the homophobia present in the treatment environment. They may need to interpret the "rules of recovery" which are sometimes put forth as the only way to get and stay sober. For example, recovery from alcoholism is posited on the notion that unless people are completely honest and open about themselves they will not be able to recover and maintain that recovery. In order to achieve stable sobriety, alcoholics must practice rigorous honesty, must take responsibility for their feelings and behavior, and must not blame others for what is happening in their lives. Over and over, the message is — no masks, no hiding of self. These premises present obvious difficulties for gay/lesbian alcoholics, and it is critically important that counselors understand those difficulties and be prepared to assist their gay/lesbian clients.

The reality for most gay people is they must continue to pass as straight in the outside world. If a gay person is a teacher, a firefighter, a clergy member, a police officer, or an employee of a large corporation, he or she runs a high risk of losing the job by coming out as a gay person. If a gay male or lesbian is married and does not wish to break up that relationship, then he or she may choose to continue passing. If a gay male or lesbian's family is likely to disown him or her if they find out, then passing would seem to be an appropriate response to that threat. And if, in spite of A.A.'s policies and traditions, the gay/lesbian alcoholic runs the risk of being rejected by a particular group for coming out, then passing is most certainly the better part of valor. What counselors can do if they can win their gay/lesbian clients' trust, is to help them make some important distinctions. Counselors can reassure clients that they can choose to not disclose their sexual orientation and still get sober. They can help clients understand that they, like all alcoholics, must be rigorously honest about their drinking and its effects on them, must start taking responsibility for their behavior and feelings, and must avoid blaming others for their drinking problems. At the same time, however, counselors can assist their clients in beginning to address homophobia which can pose a major threat to their recovery.

Part of coming to healthy terms with homophobia is for gays to realize society has the problem, not gays. It is healthy and necessary to their mental health for gay men and lesbians to place the responsibility where it belongs — not on themselves for being who they are but on a society which attacks those who do not conform to its moralistic views.

The extent of homophobia and the necessity of passing as a defense against it underscore the importance of gay/lesbian A.A. and Al-Anon meetings, accepting sponsors, knowledgeable and empathetic counselors, and treatment centers where it is safe for gay/lesbian patients and staff members to be open. These are extremely important factors because they provide gay/lesbian alcoholics with safe opportunities to be open and honest in a world that frequently refuses to permit it. Clients repeatedly report that when they speak at gay/lesbian A.A. meetings, they experience a wonderful feeling of freedom to tell their real stories, to share their true selves. And their stories often include a generous and accepting non-gay sponsor who gave them hope and held out a nonhomophobic hand; or an understanding counselor who listened, cared, and supported them in their struggle to accept their alcoholism and their gayness. This was often especially important because many gays do not have their families' support — either because they are afraid to tell them, or because they have done so and have been rejected. Passing and being selective about revealing sexual orientation are legitimate activities for gay/lesbian alcoholics in recovery.

Although coming to terms with the possibility of being bisexual or gay or lesbian is very difficult and painful, it does give people a certain advantage. As people become aware of their sexual identity, the battleground changes. Whereas before the fight was an inner one with homophobic attacks primarily directed at self, now the person can focus his or her fight on the proper target — the forces of homophobia which originate and reside in society.

PART TWO

DIRECT TREATMENT ISSUES

This section is intended to provide some useful concepts, different perspectives, and practical techniques. There are, however, no hard and fast rules about how this information should be applied. The only sure statement about this material is that it all depends — on the setting, the client, the stage of the alcoholism, the timing, and the counselor. This section offers guidelines and suggestions which counselors can incorporate into their counseling repertoire and use according to their needs and skills.

The Setting

In order to be most effective and helpful, counselors must know the strengths and limitations of the setting where they are providing service. It is important to know what the administration's attitudes and policies about homosexuality are. Is the administration supportive of quality care for sexual minority patients? Does the administration tacitly allow homophobia among its staff and administrators? Does it truly support good treatment for all gay/lesbian alcoholics? It is equally important to know the attitudes of other staff members. Are they homophobic? Are they well-informed about gay/lesbian issues or ignorant of them? Do they gossip about clients? Or do all staff treat clients and their confidential, personal issues with respect and sensitivity? Are there any openly gay/lesbian people on staff? If not, would a qualified openly gay person be hired if he or she applied for an opening? Is it safe for a gay person to be known as gay on this staff? Is it safe for a non-gay person to advocate for gays without being stigmatized in some way? Are staff members comfortable discussing sexuality in general — homosexuality in particular? If necessary, is in-service training available to help staff deal with sexuality issues? Is it or can it be provided? The answers to these and other questions can help evaluate the setting and the degree of safety provided for the gay/lesbian client. (See Appendix A.)

In addition, other specific questions need to be asked about each type of treatment setting. What are the length, intensity, type, and goal of treatment? For example, in a detoxification facility where the length of stay is short and clients are often physically ill, the primary reason for asking about sexual orientation is to be able to provide support and to facilitate appropriate referral. Another important question is, what kind of population does the detox serve? If, for example, it serves a primarily revolving-door clientele, mostly street people who know one another on the outside, it may be dangerous for a client to reveal his or her gayness to other clients.

An inpatient unit is usually different. More time for treatment, stronger bonds among clients and staff, and a staff with more advanced training work to the clients' advantage. It is often possible for clients in a reasonably non-homophobic rehabilitation unit to talk about their sexual orientation in group therapy and receive support. Interestingly, a non-homophobic atmosphere has far-reaching effects because the treatment setting feels safe to all patients, both gay and non-gay. It provides an environment where people are free to disclose all kinds of secrets that may hinder recovery.

Numerous factors can aid in creating this kind of non-homophobic, accepting atmosphere. One of the best is regularly and frequently scheduled lectures on sexuality that address gay/lesbian issues in a sensitive, direct manner. It is also helpful for staff to handle patients' responses to these lectures in a comfortable way. Staff members who are direct and at ease when discussing sexuality give all patients tacit permission to raise their specific issues when they are ready to do so. It also identifies staff persons who are safe resources for clients. Another way to help make the atmosphere feel more secure is not tolerating homophobic remarks by clients or other staff and challenging these remarks as directly and publicly as feasible. Openly gay male and lesbian staff members can also send a powerful message to clients that it is safe to be gay or lesbian in a particular rehab. In addition, these staff people can serve as excellent role models of the freedom to be oneself. Having gay/lesbian recovering alcoholics serve as A.A. contacts for clients is another way to send safety messages. They also serve as role models for the gay/lesbian clients *and* the non-gay clients, many of whom have never known a gay man or lesbian who has successfully recovered from alcoholism/chemical dependency.

Another way to help create a more non-homophobic atmosphere is to make sure the literature on the unit is written in gay-sensitive language. For example, pamphlets describing the rehab's program should not just talk about spouses or husbands and wives. These references ignore the existence of same-sex significant others and send a negative message to the gay/lesbian reader. It is important that the language acknowledge *lovers, partners,* or some other terms that are not limited to heterosexuals. In the same sense, family concepts need to include same-sex partners and friends. It is not unusual for a "roommate" of thirty years' standing to be ignored while a distant, alienated cousin is made official next-of-kin, is given visiting privileges at family times, and is chosen to be invited to the Family Group. Obviously, treatment planning and outreach efforts need to be sensitive to the often-overlooked issues of the gay/lesbian client or family member.

The halfway house setting is similar yet different from the inpatient unit. Because of the length of time people stay and because staff are frequently more closely involved with day-to-day living issues, strong bonds develop often among staff and clients. In many ways, because of the longer time period, this can be an ideal, safe setting for gay/lesbian clients to begin clarifying their sexual identity issues, if necessary. They can go to gay/lesbian A.A. meetings if they choose to and establish firmer bonds with the gay/lesbian A.A. community.

The halfway house can provide either a valuable or miserable experience for gay/lesbian alcoholics. The quality of the experience depends on the quality of the staff. The experience can indeed be a powerfully positive one if staff members learn about working with gay/lesbian clients, if they are willing to support them, if they are willing to draw reasonable boundaries for them, and if they are willing to challenge and refuse to tolerate homophobia in their house. However, these clients are likely to leave early and not get the help they need if the staff will not support the gay/lesbian client, if the staff tolerates homophobia either in themselves or in the house members, or if the staff simply denies the existence or possibility of gay or lesbian clients.

Ultimately, counselors should assess how well their particular treatment setting lends itself to helping gay/lesbian alcoholic clients. How counselors will work with their clients will depend on this assessment. If the treatment setting is homophobic, gossipy, insensitive, and not very safe, competent counselors will not reveal certain information even to other staff. They can provide clients with a sensitive ear but may have to advise them not to come out to others. If, however, the atmosphere is safe, counselors can assure clients that if they wish to self-disclose, the staff will be supportive and helpful with peers' responses. Much depends on the nature and atmosphere of the setting.

Gathering Information

In training sessions, counselors frequently ask why they should question clients about their sexual orientation — often claiming that it is an invasion of privacy and not the counselor's business. However, if the question is not posed, the gay/lesbian client may feel heterosexuality is assumed and homosexuality is possibly unacceptable in this setting. It may indicate that a treatment facility or a counselor is not sensitive to gays. Asking about sexual orientation at least presents a choice. It says the agency acknowledges that gays exist and that the counselor is comfortable enough to ask. Asking questions of all new patients can provide the first ray of hope that nonjudgmental help is perhaps available. These messages are powerful motivators for frightened gay/lesbian alcoholics and any client who is confused or frightened about any sexual identity issue. Most importantly, asking questions permits the client to be less worried about when "they" will find out. Anxiety about being "found out" is often a constant, underlying fear that gays live with and is likely to be evoked in a mainstream treatment setting. If clients are asked as a matter of course, they at least have the opportunity to confront their fears directly. Inquiring gives clients a choice about disclosing and sends a message that sexual orientation is a legitimate issue. If sexual orientation is *not* asked about, the anxiety will remain, perhaps increase, and will in some way interfere with and detract from the recovery process. Asking also addresses the issue of secret pain which, if not shared, may result in the client's feeling alienated, alone, and unique.

Thus, counselors need to take a thorough psychosocial-sexual history in a caring, relaxed manner. The most reassuring message that can be conveyed is, "This is routine; we ask everyone these questions as a matter of course. And we're okay with the answers, whatever they may be." If this message gets across, the gay/lesbian person may not feel so frightened and may begin to develop some trust. If counselors have trouble feeling relaxed and routine in asking questions about sexuality or about sexual

61

orientation, they need to be de-sensitized about this issue. One helpful technique is to practice by role-playing both counselor and client roles. It may also help to talk with a supervisor and to obtain more specific training about working with gay/lesbian clients.

Some "How-To's"

There are various ways to ask clients about their sexual orientation and their sexual experiences. One is by explaining the Kinsey Scale and then asking the client to find his or her place on it. Oftentimes, questions using the Kinsey scale and the Klein grid can form the basis for talking about fears, problems, or orientation. Another method is asking indirect questions such as, "Has sex ever been a problem for you?" or "If you could have your choice of any counselor at all and could choose from male/female, gay/straight, black/white/Hispanic, who would you choose?" Other more direct questions include, "How often do you have sexual relations? Are they satisfactory or have alcohol and drugs caused problems? Is (are) your partner(s) male or female, or do you have both?" "Who is your main sex partner (with a list of potential partners such as girlfriend/boyfriend, male/female lover, husband/wife)?" The most direct question of all would be, "What is your sexual orientation?" or "Are you homosexual, bisexual, heterosexual?"

Another standard part of taking the history is to ask about the person's sexual behavior while drinking. Often the more direct the question, the easier the answer. Thus it may be best to ask, "While you were drinking, did you have sexual relations with someone of your own sex?" Counselors need, of course, to listen very carefully to the response, whether it be shock, annoyance, embarrassment, or confusion, no reply, or too quick of a reply. By asking about and interpreting the clients' responses to the question, counselors may be able to help clients (whether gay or non-gay) reveal painful material. But it is important to avoid rushing in and reassuring the client that same-sex behavior while drinking does not mean he or she is gay. First of all, the client may or may not be gay. Second, such a response on the counselor's part could well be insulting to a gay person or at least indicative of some homophobia. Third, the client may be testing by making an initial partial admission to bisexual or homosexual actions only when drunk. To reassure prematurely can slam the door on further exploration of feelings and questions. Instead, inviting and assisting the client to explore the meanings of the experience for him- or herself is far more helpful. This latter approach is often far more reassuring in the long run.

It is also essential to ask clients whether they have ever been sexually abused — and by whom. It is important to ask *both* men and women because a number of men have been sexually abused, sometimes by women, more usually by male relatives or friends. Many women have been abused by fathers, brothers, and grandfathers; but a number (no one knows how many) have been abused by their mothers or other female relatives. Many of these men and women have lived for years with the fear that they are or will become gay or lesbian because of their early same-sex experiences. They may or may not be gay, but their unexplored fears may have contributed significantly to their misuse of alcohol. Certainly, they need to talk about such fears and be free to explore their sexual identity issues within a caring and safe atmosphere. Clients also need permission, however, to put stuff on the shelf and *not* talk about material that is deeply disturbing to them. In many ways, this becomes a matter of delicate timing and discerning judgment calls on the part of the counselor.

Although counselors may ask all the "right questions in the right way," gay/lesbian clients may not answer them truthfully — for any number of reasons. It is important, therefore, that counselors listen with "gay-sensitive" ears for other clues — depression (even though it may have many sources, it needs to be checked against other clues); never using the singular pronouns *she* or *he*, only *they;* and confused and confusing answers or vagueness about close relationships, dating patterns, significant others, socializing, and sexual behavior. If counselors sense that clients may be hiding facts or not answering honestly, the counselors need to assess their own attitudes and delivery, the client's situation, and whether or not pressing for greater openness is advisable.

Clients may or may not answer frankly, but it is important that questions be asked. Gay men and lesbians who have been in treatment repeatedly reported they felt better when their counselors asked questions that gave positive signals. Some said they answered honestly, some said they lied, but almost all said they felt better because they believed the counselors cared and they could go to these counselors if they absolutely *had* to talk to someone. The importance of asking these questions is underscored by the many gay and lesbian alcoholics who report they were never asked about their sexual orientation during treatment. As they explained, the subject of their sexual orientation was never raised, and they slipped through without receiving appropriate counseling, support, or referrals. Some of the destructive effects of such negligence are illustrated by the example of a young man who called NALGAP for help during a relapse which occurred shortly after he had completed a 28-day inpatient rehabilitation program. He explained that his sexual orientation never came up during the 28 days, and he had not felt safe to raise the issue himself. So he left this rehab without knowing there were local gay men's A.A. meetings. Although it is true he might have relapsed whether or not he knew about the gay meetings, the real issue is an ethical one. He had received shoddy, irresponsible treatment because no one assisted him with viable aftercare plans — much less with issues which were relevant to his stay on the unit. It is unethical for treatment professionals not to ask questions whose answers will enable them to provide appropriate care. It is ethical and compassionate to ask, to listen, and to respond.

Basic Treatment Information

Certain matters particular to gay/lesbian alcoholics require specific attention. The issues discussed in this section are often relevant to the recovery process and are frequently encountered when counseling gay/lesbian alcoholics. It is important that counselors have information about these issues and know how to use this information.

A Matter of Diversity

Lesbians and gay men are indeed everywhere in society and may have journeyed into treatment from diverse backgrounds, experiences, and lifestyles. The client sitting across from the counselor may have been passing as heterosexual, living as an integral part of the larger culture, and wanting to continue to do so. Or the client may have been living in a subculture with its own norms, mores, and activities that differ from those of the larger culture. Furthermore, the lesbian client and the gay male client will not have come from the same subcultures. Indeed, the gay male and lesbian subcultures are quite different.

Each has its own books, magazines, newspapers, music, activities, and interests. Each has separate and distinct mores and values. And, there is not just one lesbian or one gay male subculture; there are many smaller divisions of these subcultures. The terms *gay community* and *lesbian community* do not refer to unified, sharply definable entities. These terms do not refer to all gay men or lesbians since a number of them do not consider themselves part of a larger community. Rather, these terms refer to loose aggregates of people who are diverse in character, values, and attitudes. Members of some of these "sub-subcultures" may never mix, while some may share and work together on common social and political goals. Perhaps a primary reason for the distinctive differences between gay male and lesbian subcultures is they are determined on the basis of people's socialization as *males* and as *females*. Gay men are much more similar to non-gay men than to gay women; and lesbians are much more similar to non-lesbian women than they are to gay men.

Sober Socializing and Sober Sex

As clients begin to trust their counselors, one of the key issues that may arise is the whole question of sober socializing and sober sex. Gay/lesbian clients may say they're afraid to have sex because they fear sexual contact will upset their equilibrium and they'll drink. It is helpful for counselors to talk about internalized homophobia, the need to drink in order to make it possible to have sexual contact, and the possibility of putting sexual activity aside for a while. In fact, counselors may need to give clients permission to do so. Or counselors may have to help clients explore ways to socialize without jeopardizing sobriety. Counselors will need to address the whole issue of going to bars in a way that is very different from addressing the matter with non-gay alcoholics. It is important to understand the function of bars in some of the gay male and lesbian subcultures. Gay or lesbian bars are much more than bars; oftentimes they are the one place where a gay man or lesbian can go and be reasonably sure the other people there are also gay or lesbian. This assurance of the other people's similar sexual orientation is critically important because this is an invisible identity. Contrary to the mythology, it is not usually possible to know who is gay or lesbian just by looking at the person. They do *not* "all look alike."

Traditionally, then, gay bars have been the places where people could go and feel relatively safe in making social and/or sexual overtures to others of the same sex. The gay bars have also traditionally been the places where people would go to make contact — they were the places to meet others like oneself. Thus it just doesn't work to flatly say, "Look, if you don't want to get hit by the train, don't sit on the tracks. So don't go to bars." For many gays, that's like telling them their social life is over — that they can no longer go to what is often the only place available to meet other gays in a relatively safe atmosphere. While it seems reasonable to strongly urge newly recovering clients to stay away from bars altogether for *at least* ninety days, clients may resist such urgings. If clients are adamant about going to bars, it does not work to hit such resistance head on. Instead, counselors can be helpful by being realistic. For instance, counselors can continue to caution about the dangers while at the same time assisting their clients in figuring out ways to make going to gay bars safer — such as going to the bar with a group of other recovering alcoholics after a meeting. Whatever the outcome, counselors should not engage in a so-called "knee-jerk reaction" of saying to gay/ lesbian clients, "Don't go to the bars." Such reactions elicit resistance and indicate the counselors' lack of knowledge about an important issue. This tends to undermine counselor credibility.

One other issue relating to sober sex and socializing needs to be mentioned. As is true for some heterosexuals, some gay men, lesbians, and bisexuals are caught up in compulsive sexual behavior. Depending on how they feel about themselves and their behavior, it is possible their compulsive behavior puts them at high risk of relapse if they don't deal with it. Although this is not an issue most counselors are equipped to deal with in any depth, they may have to recognize and address it if the client's compulsive sexual behavior is enmeshed in his or her alcoholism. Probably the best course of action is to get a gay/lesbian A.A. member to talk to the client or to refer the client to a gay-sensitive therapist who knows something about alcoholism. There are also a growing number of self-help groups for sexual compulsives, most of which include gay and non-gay members.

Significant Others and Family Issues

In recent years, the alcoholism field has become increasingly aware of the need to treat not only the alcoholic but also the significant other (the person closest to the alcoholic) and other family members. Many facilities and agencies have created specific programs to provide such treatment. But probably the majority of these have not paid much attention to including gay/lesbian alcoholics' significant others (SO) and family members. Thus counselors need to consider several factors. They need to think creatively about who may be the client's SO and who may constitute the gay/lesbian person's family. For example, the gay person and his or her lover may not live together or may even live far apart. Or the SO may be an ex-lover with whom the client lives and maintains a long-term friendship. Gay or lesbian clients' extended families may consist of their friends rather than blood relatives, so counselors need to learn what friends or others are involved with their clients. By doing so, counselors may be able to determine who makes up the clients' support systems and encourage that support. Counselors may also be able to determine who the enablers are, what the clients' environments are like, and how to assist the clients with reentry issues.

Counselors need to be sensitive to another issue. It is quite possible that a person's lover or close friend is closeted and does not feel safe coming to the treatment facility or is not willing to risk disclosure by becoming involved in a group. Counselors may need to see the alcoholic and his or her lover as a couple or possibly refer them elsewhere. Or counselors may be able to help a client assist his or her lover or friend to come into the family treatment program. Such a program would need to be sensitive to and aware of the special issues involved with gay/lesbian people. Most importantly, counselors should realize gay people's ties with others can be just as powerful, just as significant and influential as the blood and marriage ties of non-gay people.

Counselors need also to be aware of potential problems and issues in regard to gay/lesbian clients' families of origin. If the agency is not sensitive to these matters, it may push for contacting the family of origin without discovering that the client has been rejected by them. Or the client may have good reason for not wanting the family to become involved because the risk of exposure is too great. Or the client may feel he or she has let down the family by being gay or lesbian; he or she may feel unable to face them or fears they will not come to the family program if asked. In these situations, counselors need to make therapeutic judgments (in consultation with the client) about what is best for the client's sobriety. But those judgments must be based on an appreciation of the sensitive nature of these matters.

Another sensitive issue may arise at times. It is quite possible the gay male or lesbian client is married, has children, and is involved with another person or persons of the same sex. Counselors must face the issue of knowing about a situation which they are not free to reveal (to the husband or wife, for instance) but which clearly affects the spouse. Counselors also need to pay close attention to the possibility of personal biases about such relationships and need to monitor their feelings and attitudes. For example, does the counselor feel strongly about the client staying in the marriage, no matter what? Or is there a subtle belief that the client should tell the spouse? Is there a feeling that the client should give up the same-sex partner(s) or behavior? Are counselors willing to consider a same-sex lover as an SO worthy of respect and in need of treatment, just like the spouse? Because this issue is a difficult and sensitive one, counselors should monitor their attitudes and act with great care, basing their treatment plans and actions on the most objective and unbiased perspectives they can muster.

It is possible that some clients will have no one. Then, it becomes especially important to find supportive contacts for them. If gay/lesbian A.A. members are available, they can help serve as support people. At the very least, counselors should contact hotlines and national organizations that can steer the client to others who can be helpful and supportive.

Parents or Children of Gays

An often overlooked issue concerns that of parents or children of gays. From time to time, the alcoholic in treatment is the parent or the child of a gay or lesbian person. In order to assist such a person, counselors first of all need to ask *every* client whether or not they have a gay or lesbian child or parent. As stated earlier, asking sends messages that counselors know such relationships exist and it is possible to talk about them with a degree of safety. Many have never told anyone and feel unique and isolated. Parents of gays may be struggling with terrible guilt, feeling they somehow caused their child's gayness. Often the first questions parents ask when they discover their child is gay is, "Where did I go wrong? What did I do wrong?" The burden of such guilt can be extremely destructive to alcoholics struggling to get sober. The same is true of the burden of anger, disappointment, shame, and confusion.

Alcoholics in treatment who are the children of gays are also likely to be struggling with their feelings toward their parents. They may be experiencing pain, fear, confusion, shame, rage, and guilt — which can be destructive to recovery efforts if they are not dealt with. And if clients are burdened by other family secrets (incest, physical violence, alcoholism, gambling), they may feel overwhelmed by the fear that "someone will discover my secret and will know how terrible I am." Double shame is more than doubly painful. These clients may also fear others will think they are gay. So most parents or children of gay or lesbian people are not likely to volunteer this information. When counselors create a safe space by asking in a caring and accepting manner, it may be possible for troubled clients to get help. Basically, counselors will provide the same help to parents and children as to gay and lesbian clients — such as dealing with feelings, accepting them, reassuring them, educating them that no one causes homosexuality, and, when appropriate, referring them to organizations such as Parents of Lesbians and Gays or other support groups. The appropriateness of referrals and counseling interventions needs to be determined on the basis of what stage clients (whether gay, lesbian, parent, or child) have reached in coming to terms with these issues. (See Stage Theories, pp. 77.)

Religious Guilt

Either when first beginning to entertain the possibility of being gay or later when trying to come to terms with being gay, many people start feeling guilty on the basis of their early religious training. People may be especially vulnerable in early sobriety because the buffer between them and their guilt has been removed. Counselors can help with this partly through their attitudes; if counselors do not view being gay as a sin but as an acceptable alternative lifestyle, then clients can at least feel supported in their struggle to resolve some of their guilt. Another means of helping is by putting gay/lesbian clients in touch with religious organizations such as Dignity (Catholic), Integrity (Episcopal), the International Conference of Gay and Lesbian Jews, the Conference of Catholic Lesbians, and the Metropolitan Community Church (Protestant). Another way is to have a non-homophobic gay/lesbian or non-gay clergyperson talk with the client and perhaps help him or her to take a Fifth Step.

Confidentiality

This issue touches on all others. It is at the heart of all decisions about trust, disclosure, and protection of sensitive information. Only one state (Wisconsin) and only about fifteen major cities have laws that specifically protect gay and lesbian people's rights.[1] Too many gay men and lesbians have lost jobs, children, places to live, and friends and family because their sexual orientation was revealed. Knowledge about the laws of each state and city is important for the creation of an informed and appropriate treatment plan. But the question of confidentiality reaches beyond knowledge of the law because homophobia runs deep and operates beyond the law. It becomes, therefore, necessary for counselors to make sure their clients' sexual orientation or their concerns about their orientation be carefully shielded from potential danger.

Counselors need to be particularly sensitive about confidentiality issues when dealing with lesbians and gay men who are parents. Lesbian and gay male parents are at very high risk of losing their children in custody battles if their sexual orientation becomes known. Added to that, if the gay/lesbian parent is alcoholic, the risks run even higher. Another very sensitive issue is the results of any HIV (for AIDS) testing on clients either before entering alcoholism treatment or during their treatment. The national press has clearly documented the negative reactions extended to people who are even suspected of having AIDS — from children being barred from schools to people being evicted from apartments and fired from jobs.

The particular aspects of confidentiality which need careful attention are twofold: staff and agency attitudes and charting. If counselors are aware of gossipy or homophobic staff, it may not be appropriate to share information about gay/lesbian clients with them. It is also important to recognize that a client's chart may be seen by people other than staff. From time to time, insurance carriers request and receive charts for review to determine whether the services claimed were in fact provided. Information about a client will possibly be known outside an agency, a matter which seriously affects confidentiality. Different facilities have various ways of dealing with this problem. One way is to not write sensitive information in the chart. Another is to have two sets of charts — one for outside agencies, the other for in-house use. Whatever way a particular facility deals with this matter, confidentiality has a special urgency to it when sexual orientation is involved.

Acquired Immune Deficiency Syndrome (AIDS)

AIDS is a special issue that cannot be ignored because it affects gay men, IV drug users, bisexual and heterosexual people, and alcoholics (whatever their sexual orientation) who are often in the high risk group because of sexual experiences while drinking and the effects of alcohol on their immune systems. AIDS cannot be ignored because it affects everyone in some way — physically, emotionally, or spiritually. AIDS cannot be ignored by people committed to providing alcoholism treatment because ignoring it violates our trust as care-givers and our responsibility as human beings.

To work knowledgeably with an alcoholic population, counselors need to understand what AIDS is. *AIDS* refers to *Acquired* (developed at some time after birth or passed from pregnant mothers to fetuses) *Immune Deficiency* (a lack or weakness in the body's defense system against many kinds of infections and cancers) *Syndrome* (a cluster of symptoms). The cause of AIDS is the HIV virus which weakens the immune system and creates the opportunity for certain diseases (known as "Opportunistic" diseases) to invade the body. The two most common that occur with AIDS are Kaposi's Sarcoma and Pneumocystis carinii pneumonia. Some people get *ARC, AIDS Related Complex*. They experience a somewhat milder version of the depression of their immune systems but are subject to a range of mild to severe illnesses. People with ARC may or may not develop AIDS. The way the AIDS virus is transmitted is by exchanges of body fluids, especially semen and blood.

Counselors need to know what their agencies' policies are towards Persons with AIDS (PWA). Are PWA's acceptable for admission? Or does the agency or institution refuse to admit anyone with AIDS or ARC? What happens if someone has an HIV positive test reading? It is critically important to know these policy factors to anticipate events and attitudes if a client discloses himself as gay, or if a client discloses him- or herself as an IV drug user or reveals a background of sexual activity while drinking which places him or her in the high risk group. If a client has AIDS, would he or she be forced to leave the unit or be placed in isolation? If the agency has a policy of admitting people with AIDS or ARC, what procedures have been established to manage these occurrences? Are there lists of standard precautions? Are they posted so all staff and all clients can read them? Is literature explaining AIDS available to all patients and staff? Do all staff receive thorough, ongoing in-service training? Is a discussion of AIDS included as a standard part of lectures on sexuality? Are safe sex practices included in the sexuality lectures? What is the agency's policy about testing for HIV? How are the findings of this test handled regarding confidentiality and the particular state's laws? Do clients have the right to refuse the test? Or will they be asked (or pressured) to leave if they refuse?

If counselors are going to provide good treatment for gay males and other clients, they need to know enough about AIDS/ARC to teach and reassure other staff and clients. The public's irrational fears about AIDS are enormously powerful, and often these fears fuel others — especially homophobia. Therefore, informed, level-headed staff are needed to teach others in order to allay some of the fears. It is important for counselors to know enough about AIDS to address the fears of the "worried well," people in high risk groups (gay men especially) who are often irrationally convinced they have or soon will have AIDS. It is equally important for counselors to be able to address the denial some people have about the risks of unsafe sex practices or sharing of needles.

Although not all fear can be banished by teaching about AIDS, education is certainly a most effective weapon. In educating others, it is best to assume people know little about AIDS. It helps to begin with the most basic information, especially how the disease is and is not transmitted because many people (including a number of gay men and lesbians) are remarkably uninformed or ill-informed — such as believing AIDS can be caught by touching someone who has it. Information about the ways alcohol and other drugs can weaken the immune system should be included in any lecture on the physical effects of alcoholism and chemical dependency. Everyone — especially gay men and bisexual men and women — should be taught about safe sex practices and the risks of unsafe sex practices.

One other aspect needs to be considered. What attitudes about sobriety do staff members and affected clients have in the face of a fatal diagnosis of AIDS? Any client who is on a treatment unit and has been diagnosed as having AIDS has to deal with the value of sobriety in the face of impending death. Other clients and staff may have to deal with that question also. All staff (from the cleaning people to the psychiatrists) should be trained in death and dying issues and their relationship to the Twelve Steps. Staff people also need to turn to one another when dealing with the inevitable stress involved in working with death and dying. The staff needs to monitor their own attitudes regarding AIDS and the ways people contract the disease to determine whether they feel gay men are paying the price for sexual promiscuity. If staff members have such attitudes, they need to refer the client to someone else or work through their feelings. Ultimately, this whole issue comes down to the same essentials: counselors need to be well-informed, aware of their own attitudes, and willing to assist clients in feasible and appropriate ways.

Whatever issues arise for individual clients, the essential truth is that failure to address and attend to them can be destructive to the clients. There is no scientific way to measure the destructiveness of such negligence. But gay/lesbian alcoholics repeatedly report how terrible it felt to have counselors ignore obvious clues about sexual orientation or tell them sexual orientation was not relevant to recovery. Being gay or lesbian involves far more than sexual orientation and raises many important life issues. Not to be acknowledged as a whole person feels terrible. It also means proper and appropriate treatment cannot be given. On the other hand, counselors who address these special issues with knowledge and sensitivity provide gay/lesbian alcoholics with the quality of treatment that can help them recover from their alcoholism/chemical dependency.

Dual Stigmas

With this discussion of special issues in mind, it is time now to consider what may be the central link between alcoholism and homosexuality. Essentially, this link is the stigma and

75

accompanying oppression that is directed at alcoholics and homosexuals.

A blackboard exercise we frequently do in training events starkly underscores the link. Participants are asked to call out every negative societal myth and reaction to "drunks" that they can think of. The list is long and unpleasant and includes such designations as "weak, sick, mentally ill, immoral, sinful, promiscuous, disgusting, repulsive, dangerous, aggressive, threatening, irresponsible, parasitic." Then, participants are asked to indicate which of these negative characteristics also apply to homosexuals. The answer is all of them — and then some. Alcoholics and homosexuals are tarred by the same brush.

A second blackboard exercise then illuminates the remarkable similarities between alcoholics' and homosexuals' responses to stigma and oppression. First, the following list is placed on the board: denial; anxiety; fear, "paranoia"; hostility, anger, rage, arrogance; guilt, shame; self-pity; depression (powerless, helpless, hopeless); fragmentation; isolation, alienation; confusion; low self-esteem. Then, participants (who are alcoholism service providers) are asked to identify the list. They state that it is a list of psychological "symptoms" of alcoholism. The fuller interpretation is that it is a list of psychological responses to the oppressive, destructive effects of alcoholism. Then, the trainer goes through this same list again, but this time the trainer points out how these are responses that homosexuals have to the oppressive and destructive effects of homophobia. When doing this, the trainer makes sure that he/she unequivocally states *homosexuality is not a disease;* but homophobia is indeed a social disease, a disease of society's attitudes, just like racism or sexism.

These, then, are psychological responses to the oppressive force of stigma — being identified with a group that is not only *different from* the mainstream but also *stigmatized, reviled,* and *ostracized* by it. These responses are intensified and are often harder to deal with because they occur in reaction to an *invisible* stigma.[2] Because neither homosexuality nor

76

abstinent alcoholism are visible, it is possible to hide these facts — as many do, at least in some situations. The problem for gay/lesbian people or anyone who is confused about sexual identity is that all too often treatment systems collude in keeping the secret, in keeping the stigma invisible. And then the treatment is incomplete and inadequate.

If these were the only ways people could respond to having a stigmatized identity, there would be little reason for people to have hope. But such is not necessarily the case, as anyone familiar with A.A. can testify.[3] Coming to terms with, learning to manage, and integrating a stigmatized identity ultimately is a positive experience. The acquisition of health and recovery from these mental and emotional states seem to follow a common path — awareness, admission, acceptance (surrender), and reconstruction. This path to recovery from the oppressive and destructive force of stigma, this transformation of identity, is discussed and explained in the following section.

The Stages of Forming a Gay/Lesbian Identity

At this point, we wish to present a theoretical model of the process of forming a gay male or lesbian identity. Although this is just a construct, it offers a perspective that can assist counselors in interpreting and clarifying what gay clients may be experiencing. It is a perspective that can help counselors answer such questions as, What might I expect? What am I seeing, experiencing with this client? What does this mean? How can I help my client deal with sexual identity issues? In addition, the model can profitably be applied to the process of forming an identity as a recovering alcoholic. The model allows us to describe, explore, and understand the dynamics of learning to manage and integrate gay/lesbian identity issues and recovering alcoholic identity issues and the dynamics created by the interconnections between the two processes. In addition, it provides a perspective on the issues, problems, and concerns that can occur at any point in these processes; thus, the model is a valuable tool in planning and guiding treatment strategies.

The model presented here is primarily an amalgam of two models, with influences from others.[4] One was created in 1971 by William Cross, a black psychologist, in order to explore the process by which a "Negro" develops an identity as a black.[5] In essence, Cross describes how people *transform* their identities from a negative, stigmatized state to a positive state where they refuse to accept the validity of the stigma; they then take pride in their identity. In 1979, Australian psychologist Vivienne Cass constructed her model of "how a person acquires a homosexual identity" on the basis of her empirical study.[6] Other influences are Barbara Ponse's study of lesbian identity issues and David R. Rudy's investigation of the process of "becoming alcoholic."[7] No one has studied the applicability of these models to the *dual* processes of dealing with two stigmatized identities (lesbian or gay male and alcoholic) at one time. The interconnections have long interested both of us, and now Emily McNally is devoting her doctoral dissertation to a study of the processes lesbian recovering alcoholics engage in as they manage and integrate their two stigmatized identities. Thus our discussions and explorations of these processes inform and shape the model we use. This model is based on Cross' five stage structure; draws extensively on Cass' ideas, findings, and explanations; and is tailored to alcoholism treatment by our experiences and findings.

Although this model contains five stages that suggest they are distinct entities, they are not. One stage merges into another; and a person may move back and forth between stages or may, while in one stage, have an experience that ordinarily occurs in a different stage. Furthermore, movement within the model is much more fluid than it is possible to indicate. For the sake of clarity, the model is presented in a linear and ordered fashion as follows:

1. Description of the stage as it pertains to lesbians/gay men.
2. Discussion of the similarities to the alcoholism recovery process.
3. Discussion and exploration of the interfaces among gay/lesbian identity issues, alcoholism, and treatment.

It is important to recognize the process being described here takes place over a long period of time, sometimes over a whole lifetime. Some people stay in one stage all their lives, and some of them do just fine in that stage. It may be helpful, therefore, for counselors to recognize they serve as one small link in a long chain of events and experiences. Dealing with the misery of alcoholism and becoming a recovering alcoholic is a long and complex process. Contending with the grinding oppression of homophobia and learning to accept and integrate their identity as lesbians or gay men is also a long and even more complex process. Even though helping professionals can only play a small part in such lengthy and complicated processes, the part they do play is often critically important. To provide clients with warmth, acceptance, and safety is to provide them with sanctuary, with an opportunity to gather together their forces and choose life.

Stage One: Pre-Encounter

People in this stage essentially see themselves as belonging to the mainstream. Their values are those of the mainstream. The referent for people who may be gay/lesbian is heterosexuality; they see themselves as heterosexual. The referent for people who may be alcoholic is social drinking; they see themselves as social drinkers. The key defense at this point is denial. For people who might be gay, internalized homophobia is very strong, and most have a great need not to know and not to discover or encounter any disconcerting information about their sexuality. The same dynamic is true for those who might be alcoholic: they desperately need to *not* know their drinking is different from that of mainstream people who drink socially. Counselors should always consider how much people have invested in "not knowing," in preventing others and particularly the self from discovering the truth.

At some point in this stage many people begin to sense something about them is diffcrent. Often this may be a subtle feeling that they are not "like the others," that other people seem at ease while they are not. Awareness of such feelings can and often does create a great deal of confusion and anxiety. Many people try to resolve their feelings by attempting to discover what these hints of difference might mean. Frequently they will read or will ask another person about a "friend." If what they find is negative ("homosexuals are sick," "alcoholics are disgusting"), they may slam the door on further exploration and retreat into even greater denial. They deny that homosexuality (or alcoholism) has any personal meaning for them.

Cass' term for how people stop the process from going any further is *foreclosing*.[8] There are numerous strategies of foreclosure that effectively block further information or movement. Using alcohol and other drugs is often a major one and if the use becomes heavy or addictive, the denial in response to homophobia is joined by that of alcohol and other drugs. Other foreclosure tactics may be to refuse to "hear" any more information about the subject, inhibit sexual activity (become asexual), marry, pursue a course of hypersexual heterosexuality, pray, seek a cure, or rationalize and redefine the feelings and behavior ("We're just friends," "I was drunk and didn't know what I was doing"). Whatever the specific strategy for foreclosing, the power of denial is tremendous. People have an enormous investment in being okay in the eyes of the world and themselves. Their psychic survival depends on denial and any other defense that helps them block the terrifying knowledge of who they are or might be. It is not surprising that foreclosure strategies play an important role in the various stages of identity formation.

If people in this stage come to treatment because they've hit bottom with their alcohol or drug problem and something has broken through their denial, their defenses against knowing they are gay are likely to be and remain intact. Even when not drinking, they do not see themselves as gay males or lesbians. If the treatment staff strongly suspect that these clients are gay, push hard enough, and somehow manage to break through the defense system, they risk pushing an already frightened and vulnerable person over the brink into a pit of homophobic shame. It is possible through such confrontation to evoke a "homosexual panic" in a person who is unconsciously terrified of his or her homosexual feelings. Gays who have suffered this kind of treatment report going back out to drink away the horror of this forced and unskilled confrontation. Obviously, defenses exist for very important psychological reasons and need to be regarded with respect.

If counselors shouldn't push, what should they do? They should routinely ask all clients what their sexual orientation is and accept the answer, whatever it may be. This action sends positive messages that the facility relates to sexual orientation issues in a matter of fact manner. Having open gay men and lesbians on the staff sends messages that it's safe for clients to be who they are. It is also helpful to have gay/lesbian recovering alcoholics visit the agency on a regular basis and to have them speak regularly at in-house A.A. meetings. These actions are important for two particular reasons: they signify the agency's acceptance of sexual orientations other than heterosexuality, and positive role models are extremely helpful. The importance of this becomes evident if one tries to imagine an alcoholic attempting to get sober without ever meeting any successfully recovering alcoholics. Even if no gay/lesbian people are available, non-gay counselors can serve as positive role models of non-homophobic attitudes.

In addition, it is possible to sow seeds directly. Counselors can make sure books on homosexuality are clearly visible among other books in their offices. A list of gay/lesbian A.A. meetings should be posted along with the list of other A.A. meetings. A good, clear lecture on sexuality that includes homosexuality as an acceptable alternative lifestyle provides

81

positive messages. Also, having openly gay/lesbian alcoholics speak regularly at in-home A.A. meetings can be reassuring to clients who are confused and frightened. It is also likely to smoke out homophobia among the other clients and give counselors a chance to deal with it openly (just as they would with racist remarks). Seeing counselors deal openly and firmly with homophobia can be reassuring to those who may be struggling with feelings of being different. Counselors should not tell clients in this stage that they should go to a gay/lesbian A.A. meeting. Such a recommendation implies to clients that they are seen as homosexual. Such an implication can be terrifying to the person in Stage One because his or her investment is in being seen and seeing themselves as heterosexual. In addition, people whose counselors sent them to such meetings while they were in this stage later reported they felt overwhelmed and extremely threatened by the experience.

There are exceptions. If clients exhibit confusion, conflict, or guilt when discussing their drinking behavior or express great doubt about their ability to get sober but can't specify the reasons, counselors might suspect the possibility of conflicts about sexual identity issues. Counselors can help clients disclose or at least help them entertain the possibility that their conflict is what keeps getting them drunk. If counselors feel the need for assistance in doing this or feel inadequate to the task, they might ask a gay/lesbian recovering alcoholic to come in and talk with the client. Such sessions are difficult to conduct and must be handled with skill and sensitivity. Sometimes, taking such risks with clients can help save a life. Counselors need to be very clear with themselves about their reasons for pushing or confronting a client, and it is usually a good idea for counselors to discuss such a proposed action with another professional or with a gay/lesbian person before carrying it out. If counselors do carry out some kind of confrontation, it is critically important that they be able to effect some closure. Perhaps one of the most helpful methods is to assure clients that once they have taken at least a brief look at their behavior and feelings, they can legitimately put matters on the shelf until they are able to achieve longer term sobriety and consequent stability.

Perhaps the most significant aspect of Stage One, and the one that always needs to be kept in mind, is it is a stage of *not knowing*. Furthermore, through their denial, it is possible for people to remain in this stage throughout their lives, never consciously questioning or "knowing" what their sexual identity really is, never knowing who they really are. Others move on to the second and subsequent stages. It is important for counselors to realize that while some of their clients may move into Stage Two while they are in treatment, many will probably not do so until they have been sober for several years. It is especially helpful to make sure clients have good aftercare treatment and they are in contact with counselors who are gay-sensitive. The importance of good referrals cannot be overstressed.

If and when they make the transition, others may be puzzled by what appears to be a sudden, often inexplicable shift — seemingly these people have suddenly become gay. Familiarity with this model and with alcoholism recovery provides a more reasonable explanation for this phenomenon. As people get and remain sober, they begin to come out of the fog. They gradually become aware of their surroundings and their selves in relation to those surroundings. They begin getting in touch with their feelings. Their awareness of themselves and reality and their ability to deal with their reality tend to increase. As recovering alcoholics who are in Stage One begin *encountering* hints about their sexuality, they may start being able to face and explore these hints rather than run from them.

Stage Two: Encounter

People enter Stage Two when they *encounter* somebody or something that breaks through their denial. This may occur as an accumulated result of their reading and conversation if the clues they come upon are positive, such as discovering a reassuring book like *Loving Someone Gay*, by Don Clark. Or they may have an emotional encounter or experience with a person, a book, a play, or a movie that leads them to look at the world and their place in it a little differently. This awareness may occur gradually, over a long period of time, through a series of small encounters. Or it may occur through one, big encounter that may jolt or shock people into new awareness. It may be a shattering experience. It is always an important one. It has the capacity to turn people's worlds upside down. One reaction may be "God help me, maybe I am one!" Another may be, "What will happen to me now? What will my life be like now? How will I deal with these changes in my life?"

As William Cross explains, Stage Two really consists of two parts — the encounter and the consequent reinterpretation of the person's world in light of the new awareness.[9] The encounter or discovery introduces people to a different reality where they often experience intense feelings of alienation, fear, and confusion as they struggle to learn how to live within this new reality. As Cass notes, the process of homosexual identity formation begins when people give *personal meaning* to their encounter with the notion of homosexuality.[10] Thus their tasks are to resolve the question, "Who am I?" and to find new referents (values) and meanings for this new state of affairs.

The basic defensive postures that people assume in response to the feelings aroused by these experiences are bargaining and rationalizing to put off or alter reality to make it bearable. For example, alcoholics who are in Stage Two may bargain with themselves by saying, "I'll only drink on weekends" or "I'll change brands." Or they may rationalize their drinking by thinking, "Well, I'm not that bad" or "I can stop any time I want to." Gays who are in this stage may bargain with themselves by thinking their feelings or behavior are only temporary, a phase that will pass. Or they may think, "Maybe I'm bisexual" (meaning their feelings and behavior are not really homosexual). Or they may rationalize, "I was drunk and didn't know what I was doing." "I didn't initiate what happened. The other person came on to me." "I'm different — I (Mary) just happen to love Sally who just happens to be a woman."

While people in this stage may be experiencing new feelings and behaviors, because of homophobia (society's and their own) they cannot easily accept the label and the identity. For some people, the process of working through the feelings and coming to terms with the new label and identity can be relatively brief and fairly mild, as is the process for some alcoholics who have minimal trouble with accepting their alcoholism. But for many, the process of accepting the new label and identity entails an often protracted and painful struggle with the self and society. In the course of these struggles, people are likely to experience strong feelings of alienation ("Where do I belong if I am this way?"), fear ("How will I learn to live with this new identity?"), and confusion ("Who am I anyway?").

In reaction to the pain and difficulty of this stage, people may foreclose in a variety of ways. They may go back into the denial of Stage One, or they may stop their progress towards the next stage by continuing to bargain and rationalize. Alcoholics may keep changing brands and vowing to quit tomorrow. People struggling with their sexual identity may continue to see themselves as *really* heterosexual or view their behavior as a special case. They may perceive their behavior and feelings as bisexual rather than homosexual. They may seek professional help in order to get cured. They may isolate themselves by having nothing to do with anyone who is or even appears to be gay. Or they may isolate in couples. In any event, people who foreclose in this stage do not come to terms with the label or the identity. They cannot integrate who they may really be, yet they cannot be fully at ease because they cannot be who they may wish they could be — a "normal" heterosexual.

In this stage, people who are struggling with their sexual identity are probably most vulnerable to rejection and humiliation. If they enter treatment while in this stage, they will tend to protect themselves against any perceived threats by any means available. They may lie, they may deliberately mislead others, they may retreat behind a cloud of confusion, they may rationalize every attempt by others to get at their real experience, or they may isolate themselves from others. Whatever route they take, they will defend themselves against the perceived terror of discovery. They may know the awful truth about themselves, but God forbid that anyone else should know.

A fairly small number of people react to this discovery about the self by feeling they are somehow special and different. Occasionally a client will act flamboyantly or seem to flaunt his or her sexual orientation. In such instances, counselors can be helpful by being very clear, concrete, and specific about what behavior is acceptable and what is not. But clients who have a sexual identity "secret" are much more common. These people may appear very "together," high-functioning, and aloof. Or many in this stage tend to be withdrawn, depressed, frightened, and extremely troubled when in treatment.

If clients admit to concerns about sexual identity issues when they are questioned at intake or later, counselors can be directly supportive and can help in a number of ways. Counselors need to be guided by the same sensitivity they use with alcoholics in this stage who are often unable to accept the label and identity of *alcoholic*. They do not push people to label themselves before they can tolerate such an action. Therefore, when discussing matters with clients in this stage, it is important to use language like *sexual identity* or *feelings about your sexuality* rather than *homosexual* or *gay* or *lesbian*. Gentle methods of encouraging clients are also helpful, such as: "It must be hard for you to talk about this." "What would it mean to you if you *were* gay (or lesbian)?" "Could you explain a little more about what you're feeling?" The techniques counselors use to help people discuss whatever is difficult for them are appropriate in this situation also. So, too, are all the other considerations like timing and joining clients' resistance. In terms of timing, the most help a counselor can sometimes give is to be a safe person to talk to and to advise that sexual identity issues take time and often benefit from being put on the shelf for awhile. Joining the resistance may also involve agreeing that this subject is difficult to discuss and perhaps should be put aside for the time being. If counselors and clients do, in fact, put these issues aside, it is imperative that clients receive appropriate specialized referrals for their aftercare treatment.

Those who do not admit problems or worries about sexual identity issues but seem troubled by a secret are of greater concern. The majority of people who are in Stage Two probably fall into this category. Direct confrontation is not likely to get at these secrets. If the intake and an in-depth psychosocial-sexual history do not bring out information about what is troubling these clients, counselors should be supportive in a general way and not press the clients. The ways of reaching and helping these clients will tend to be the indirect, such as sexuality lectures, visitors and speakers from gay/lesbian A.A. groups, prominently displayed lists of gay/lesbian A.A. meetings, openly available literature on sexual identity issues, and an overall non-homophobic attitude in the treatment setting. In addition, referral to gay-sensitive aftercare becomes especially important.

In addition to these indirect ways of signalling clients about the safety of their surroundings, counselors need to directly address issues of confidentiality and trust. Because people in Stage Two feel so vulnerable and so uncertain about their identity and their safety, it is critical to reassure them that if they risk disclosing their secrets to the counselor, their confidentiality will be respected and indeed actively protected. This is important because a number of people in this stage are still involved, at least partly, in heterosexual lifestyles, and many may still be married, with or without children. One approach is to tell a client whatever is said in one-to-one sessions will be kept confidential. Certainly, counselors should clarify what the boundaries of confidentiality are: Is material shared with all other staff members, just with the immediate supervisor, or just with the medical director? A helpful technique is to tell clients, "If you want to discuss this issue, I will not put it in the notes." A counselor can underscore this statement by putting his or her pen on the table. At the very least, counselors need to be clear and direct with clients about confidentiality. They need to convey their understanding of how important confidentiality is. For instance, it is important a married woman or man know the counselor has an appreciation of the possible dangers and complications inherent in their situation.

In this stage, as men and women begin to encounter or discover their sexual identity, even if only to themselves and even if only very tentatively, they have begun the process of coming out, the process of admitting to and owning their gay or lesbian orientation. Some of them will never come out of the closet any further than admitting to themselves. Many will come out in selected places with selected others but will remain primarily closeted. Some will come out full force, sometimes with destructive results. Some will come out and live as openly as possible, committed to the belief that it is important to be out in order to be free and to provide role models and leadership. Whatever a client may do, it is important for counselors to realize that coming out is a process, it may take a lifetime, and coming out in treatment may be the worst or the best thing a client can do — depending on the client, the staff, and the circumstances.

The Encounter Stage is critical to gay males' and lesbians' development of a more positive gay/lesbian identity, for it marks the beginning of their recovery from external and internalized homophobia. This same stage is critical to alcoholics who begin their road to recovery. Alcoholics must encounter something which breaks through their denial, discover their condition, admit to its existence, recognize it has personal meaning for their lives, and begin to reinterpret their lives according to this new knowledge. In terms of the A.A. program, this is taking the First Step. They have a sense of hope (as in the Second Step of the A.A. program) and if they can accept

— even a little — who they really are, people can move ahead to Stage Three. If they cannot, they may go back into the denial of Stage One or stay stuck in the restricted and often isolated position of Stage Two.

Above all else, counselors need to understand and remember people who are in Stage Two are perhaps more frightened and certainly more vulnerable than in any other stage. They have just tentatively entered into an unfamiliar country, but they have no map. This is even more threatening because the majority of the people in this country don't want them there and they don't speak the language. People in this stage feel threatened, frightened, confused, alienated, and terribly vulnerable to rejection and humiliation. They need support, protection, understanding, compassion, and acceptance. They do not need to be and should not be confronted, pressured into self-disclosure, gossiped about, pushed to disclose in group, or in any way forced to expose themselves to others. People in Stage Two are ripe for leaving treatment prematurely; many do because they feel pressured or because they are not receiving the support they need. Kindness and compassion can make all the difference; these qualities can enable a person to stay in treatment and get the help he or she needs.

Stage Three: Immersion/Emersion.

"Oh, brave new world, that has such people in it!"

— William Shakespeare

This is often the reaction of people who step into Stage Three. They discover others like themselves and are often either enchanted by the discovery or at least heartened by it. One common reaction is, "Maybe it's okay to be gay." With this, they enter into the first of the two parts of this stage. Many, if not most, immerse themselves in a gay male or lesbian world, whether an actual world or community or one constructed from reading. They tend to obsessively explore the meanings and behaviors of these new worlds and idealize all that is gay or lesbian. For example, famous gay male and lesbian artists,

89

writers, movie actors, and politicians are identified and named with the same delight that alcoholics express when discovering similar people who have recovered from alcoholism.

The other side of this coin is the tendency to denigrate all that is heterosexual. Many gay men and lesbians in this part of Stage Three are likely to dehumanize heterosexuals (for example, by calling them "breeders") and view the "straight" world as inferior (insensitive, power-hungry, uncaring). These actions are part of a partial or complete withdrawing from the mainstream, a turning inward and to peers, in order to begin sorting out and reshaping values and finding new referents for the self. This tendency to withdraw can also be counterbalanced at times by a need to confront the mainstream "other." Whatever form it may take, much of the process is geared to labelling others in an either/or fashion to clarify personal identity. Counselors may note a striking similarity to the experiences of alcoholics who immerse themselves in A.A. and look down on "Earth People."

People in this part of Stage Three tend to experience two major feelings — pride bordering on arrogance and great anger. At this point, many gays begin to feel tremendous rage against the heterosexual world for oppressing them, for demanding that gays hide and feel ashamed of their sexual orientation. The arrogance helps protect them against the tremendous pain of rejection. The anger is most certainly in response to both external and internalized homophobia.

Immersion can take many forms. Often, the very tentative and confused "trying out" of possible gayness that can characterize Stage Two gives way to active investigation of what being a gay male or lesbian can mean. A number of people in this stage may get involved in a lot of sexual experimentation and many relationships. Many people seek places where other gay/lesbian people congregate. Although these may include social or political clubs, often the most common, if not the only, place is the gay bar. If gay males and lesbians in this stage already have problems with drinking, immersing themselves in the gay bar scene can have potentially devastating consequences.

In this stage many gays leave their hometowns and move to the "gay ghettoes" in urban areas, immersing themselves and isolating themselves from non-gays. Another form of immersion is adopting, indeed heightening, the stereotypical behavior ascribed to gay men or lesbians. Men may assume more effeminate mannerisms, and women may adopt more masculine mannerisms. This behavior is often an assertion of self—"I am different and I'm proud of it" — and a challenge of mainstream values. This behavior is often viewed by heterosexuals as gays flaunting their gayness. Somewhat opposite behavior also can occur: if people are already in stable relationships, they may choose to immerse themselves even more in the relationship and their existing social circle and simply isolate themselves from larger society.

Whatever behavior occurs during this stage, the essence of immersion is an attitude, a perspective. It is the filter of gayness that everything is viewed through and measured by — is the other person gay or lesbian? Are others committed to gayness? Will non-gays be present at social functions? Who is gay or lesbian, who is not? Similarly, alcoholics who are in this part of the stage tend to evaluate all facets of life in relation to their alcoholism — Is the other person recovering? Are other people in the program? Will they serve alcohol at this function? The immersion part of this stage serves an extremely significant function; it is the process that people use to gather the information and acquire the attitudes and feelings that enable them to start integrating their gayness and/or their alcoholism.

It may be helpful at this point to refer back to the section on special issues presented earlier in this chapter. In particular, the discussion of lifestyles and gay bars can be helpful to understanding the Immersion Stage.

If people foreclose in this stage, they may define themselves as gay or lesbian but stay immersed in a small, rigidly defined subculture and isolated from the larger culture. This behavior can be compared to that of some alcoholics who foreclose at this stage of their recovery; they may be sober many years, but they still attend eight to ten A.A. meetings a week and center their lives around A.A., excluding other activities. Such foreclosure may work for them, but it tends to limit their worlds.

Certain problems may arise if gay men or lesbians enter treatment while in this stage. Many of them are struggling with a double dose of anger: the defensive anger of the alcoholic, and the defensive anger of the gay/lesbian person who has become sharply aware of the pain and injustice of homophobia and oppression. Though they may admit to being gay, they may act sullen and refuse to talk about the matter. They may be aggressive and tell counselors to mind their business. They may say things like, "What do you know? You could never understand me because you're not gay!" or "You'd drink too, if you were gay!"

Even seasoned counselors report they sometimes feel buffaloed by such challenges. It is helpful to note the similarity to other resistant statements common to alcoholics such as, "You can't understand me because you're not an alcoholic" or "You'd drink too if you had a job, a spouse, and a life like mine." Essentially, the same kinds of therapeutic responses work in all these situations — counselors can either join the resistance, or counselors can agree they probably don't fully understand but they can offer assistance, are willing to listen, and will try to understand better.

Some gay men and lesbians in this stage may act out in ultra stereotypical ways, using exaggerated mannerisms and attitudes — limp wrists, lisping, acting tough. In this way, they throw down the gauntlet to those around them, daring others to accept them. Another client may throw a group into an uproar by describing sadomasochistic experiences in great detail. Another may act seductively and make provocative sexual remarks to other clients.

It is important for the staff to keep cool in the face of such defiant behavior. Counselors need to remember to not take such behavior personally. Such behavior is irritating and may stir up the homophobia of even the staunchest supporter of gay/lesbian rights. Tolerance and understanding are the watchwords here, but firmness and refusal to be bullied are also necessary so counselors can help clients set limits on uncontrolled behavior. The best move is to face clients head-on about their behavior, help them investigate its meanings, and draw boundaries around what is and is not acceptable in the particular program. Most importantly, counselors should try to help clients temper their rage, so they can stay in treatment.

Another reaction and form of behavior common to this part of the stage is the pink cloud phenomenon: some gay/lesbian people who have discovered "gay is great" and have immersed themselves in their gayness may want to announce this news to everyone they know. This may or may not be a good idea. Though the desire to share this news with everyone may be motivated by joy, it can also be motivated by anger and needs to be examined. A number of gay/lesbian people in this stage want to tell their families, their friends, their fellow-workers, indeed the whole world they are gay.

The gay person wanting to share all is strikingly similar to the newly-recovering alcoholic who suddenly wants the whole world to know this wonderful fact. Such decisions often reflect poor judgment and poor reality testing about the possible consequences. Since alcoholics in early recovery tend to be confused and not exercise good judgment, counselors may need to help them evaluate their decisions to tell all and to tell it all at once. Acting as advocates and guides, counselors may also have to counsel their gay/lesbian clients to plan and carefully pace their coming out of the closet and help them think through the consequences and risks.

If people do not foreclose in the first part of this stage and manage to move forward, they gradually begin to come to terms with their feelings and circumstances. They begin to *emerge* from the either/or, oversimplified view of the world and are able to begin, as Cross puts it, "synthesizing . . . rage with reason."[11] In the immersion part of Stage Three, people's feelings tend to run them; in the emersion part, people gain increasing awareness of and control over their feelings and behavior. If they enter treatment while in the emersion part, they are likely to still be angry, but more controlled in their expression of that anger and less likely to be openly defiant and confrontive.

Stage Four: Internalization

People who move into this stage have begun to accept rather than just acknowledge or tolerate their being gay or lesbian. They have begun to internalize, to own their gay male or lesbian identity — just as recovering alcoholics who are in this stage have begun to accept, not just tolerate or be enamored of, their identity as alcoholics. Essentially, people in this stage must:

- come face-to-face with their new identity;
- come to terms with the reality of their identity by recognizing and acknowledging that they do not belong to the mainstream;
- evaluate and reinterpret their values, roles, and interpersonal environment.

Oftentimes this stage is characterized in part by a feeling of disenchantment: "Okay, so I'm a gay man or a lesbian. Now what?" They descend from the pink cloud and come back down to earth and reality. Different people react in different ways. Some gays reject the mainstream and pull back from it because they feel they can never belong as accepted members. Others stay immersed in the gay or lesbian subcultures, essentially stuck in a state of contempt and hatred for the heterosexual world and in a simplistic, either/or frame of mind. Others grow from their experiences and become more satisfied with themselves. They progress to a state of psychological gayness, but do not go beyond that to reintegrate themselves in the larger world. Some lesbians and gay men internalize their acceptance of who they are, make a commitment to life, and move to Stage Five.

People who go through Stage Four are likely to experience three particular emotions common to this stage: guilt, rage, and grief. Feelings of depression may also accompany these. Some people raised in formal religions may feel guilty because homosexuality is viewed as a sin by the larger culture and by most churches. Others may feel guilty for their sexual behavior while drinking. They may feel guilty for disappointing their parents by not being heterosexual, not providing grandchildren, and therefore not being acceptable. Or if gay males or lesbians are parents, they may feel guilt for "inflicting this burden" on the children. If these feelings are accompanied by guilt about alcoholism, their force is compounded and people may end up feeling guilty just for "being."

People may also feel very angry at the unfairness of experiencing such guilt simply for being who they are. Many continue to experience rage at the reality of having to live as a stigmatized person in a harsh and unaccepting world. Oftentimes, however, people channel their anger into political and social activism and fight the injustices and cruelties of a homophobic system. Such activism is often a source of pride that can serve to motivate people in their growth process.

In addition to anger, many lesbians and gay men experience grief and sadness over the loss of the great American dream of belonging to the mainstream. At this stage, gay men and lesbians are coming to terms with the truth that they are, in fact, homosexuals — and as such they can never fully belong to the larger society of heterosexuals. They cannot even hold hands with a same-sex partner in a public place without evoking raised eyebrows. If heterosexual people know or even think they know someone is gay or lesbian, many will respond in particular ways to the gay man or lesbian (for example, staring at the person, making homophobic remarks, moving away physically). The truth is that gay men's and lesbians' experience of the world is different from heterosexuals' experience,

95

because gay men and lesbians are in fact different. And no matter how closeted, no matter how invisible they may choose to be — they know.

The mourning process occurs for gay men and lesbians just as it does for alcoholics who mourn the loss of "normal" drinking and being a "normal" social drinker. Gay/lesbian alcoholics must contend with a double dose of grief, and counselors need to recognize this, acknowledge it, and try to help clients deal with it. For gay/lesbian alcoholics, sometimes just knowing another person who has some sense of the grief can be incredibly helpful in the struggle to deal with it. Ultimately, this loss of innocence tends to strengthen people, but rarely do people go through it willingly or gratefully. And such is likely to be the case with gay/lesbian alcoholics.

If lesbians or gay men are in this stage when they are in treatment, they may (like those in Stage Three) hurl such challenges as, "You can't possibly understand — you're not gay!" Or they may be loaded with guilt over unresolved conflicts about the unacceptability of being gay and their belief that they have a right to live as they choose. Some may have escaped into socially sanctioned behavior such as marriage, but feel guilty because when they drank, they acted upon their homosexual desires.

Much of what counselors can do for gay/lesbian clients in this stage is to not take the anger personally, to be supportive in regard to the guilt, and to respect and assist with the mourning. If a gay/lesbian sensitive clergyperson is available, he/she may be helpful to the client. Counselors may be able to help clients work through some of the guilt and anger by pointing out the promise of being "gay, proud, and sober." Giving gay/lesbian clients appropriate information to read may help, and assisting them to meet healthy recovering gay/lesbian alcoholics can provide hope. Ultimately, the same perspective is true for all recovering alcoholics — only by being sober can you find your way and yourself. It is especially important at this stage to refer clients (if possible) to gay/lesbian A.A. meetings.

Much has been said about grief, loss, and anger in this stage. But this is also a time of developing and getting in touch with a growing sense of pride. This pride is often a motivating force in people's being active in gay and lesbian causes; often it is a pride strongly flavored by anger. This is a state of being that tends to be constructive for people because they are beginning to learn to channel their anger into constructive, positive efforts. This stage is a time of internalization of new, more positive values based on working through grief, loss, and guilt, and the claiming of self.

Stage Five: Synthesis/Commitment

After successfully struggling with difficult and major issues in the preceding stage, people in this stage accept being gay or lesbian. They are able to feel pride about their identity. They have synthesized their experiences, worked through much of their internalized homophobia, and integrated being gay or lesbian into their personalities. That is, they have reached a point where being gay or lesbian is one part of their overall identity, one aspect of their self. Their feelings tend to be, "Society has a problem because it's homophobic. But that's not my problem. I'm me, and I'm okay; and you're okay."

Usually, by this stage, people have worked through much of their guilt and grief and have channelled their anger into a commitment to working for the betterment of other gays in some constructive activity. They have a positive sense of their gay male or lesbian identity and tend to see the world as divided less into gay/non-gay, more into supportive/nonsupportive. For the most part, gay men and lesbians at this stage are out of the closet in most places and can permit who they really are to be seen and known. They have reached a state of self-actualization which is quite different from that of Stage Three. This contrast may be compared to the difference between the frantic sobriety of early recovery and the serene sobriety of later recovery achieved by working the A.A.

program. People tend to be more at choice, more balanced, more centered, and more at peace with themselves.

If gay males or lesbians are in this stage, then usually only their alcoholism is relevant in treatment. This does not mean that their being gay or lesbian has no bearing on their treatment plan or their aftercare planning (getting in touch with the significant other, determining the best kinds of A.A. meetings to attend). But when they tell counselors that being gay or lesbian does not present any particular problem for them, they mean it.

One word of caution is in order here: it is tempting sometimes to draw on the ease and expertise of gays who have accepted themselves to learn more about what being gay or lesbian means and to employ them as role models for other gays who may be struggling with their sexual identity. While a little of this may be okay, gays and lesbians in Stage Five should not be used as counselors for others who are not so far along in their struggles with their sexual identity. Counselors always need to keep in mind that Stage Five people are probably "way back there" with regard to their alcoholism and need to be treated like the beginners they are.

The Importance of the Model

We have presented a five-stage model of the formation of gay male and lesbian identity. Primarily, we have done so to provide counselors with a logical, understandable way of perceiving gay/lesbian people who are alcoholics. Counselors may or may not be in a position to do many of the things that were discussed, but being people who are *there* for gay/lesbian clients makes an enormous difference to these clients. Knowing this model and some of the information relevant to it may help counselors aid and support their gay/lesbian alcoholic clients in lifesaving ways. Most people do not take either the time or trouble to learn or care about gay/lesbian alcoholics. Rather, most people are passively — sometimes actively — hostile towards them. When counselors care enough to learn, to understand, to reach out, and to help, gay/lesbian recovering alcoholics sense and respond to the positive messages that counselors are willing to assist in healing. This is the gift that caring counselors give to their gay/lesbian clients.

PART THREE

RESOURCES

Knowing how and where to refer clients depends on counselors developing a network of available gay-sensitive referrals and resources and keeping updated lists. Part of this network will consist of other agencies that offer assistance to gays, such as medical treatment. Another part of the network should consist of personal contacts with gay-sensitive non-gay members of A.A., gay/lesbian members of A.A., gay-sensitive therapists, and non-alcoholic gay/lesbian people. If there are colleges in the area, there may be gay groups on campus. There may also be gay/lesbian switchboards, political groups or caucuses, and social groups in many urban areas and within organizations and occupational groups (e.g., social workers, psychiatrists). The best overall resource listing is the *Gayellow Pages* (see page 104).

What follows is a list of the resources we believe will be most helpful to counselors.

National Association of Lesbian and Gay Alcoholism Professionals (NALGAP)

General Correspondence/Membership:

NALGAP
1208 East State Boulevard
Fort Wayne, IN 46805
(219) 483-8280

Clearinghouse/Library/Bibliography/Directory:

NALGAP
204 West 20th Street
New York, NY 10011
(212) 807-0634

NALGAP is a non-profit organization whose activities include forming communication and support networks for gay and lesbian alcoholism professionals, improving treatment for lesbian and gay alcoholics, and assisting alcoholism agencies and professionals to help their gay and lesbian clients. NALGAP publishes the *NALGAP Directory of Facilities and Services* which lists agencies and individuals who are, *by self-report,* gay and lesbian-sensitive. It also publishes the *NALGAP Bibliography,* the only comprehensive, annotated bibliography on alcoholism and lesbians and gay men. In addition, NALGAP acts as a clearinghouse for many unpublished papers.

The national NALGAP office also supplies information, consults with treatment and educational agencies, provides trainers, and makes referrals when appropriate for those who call or write. It is an excellent resource for people interested in providing quality care for clients, learning more about gay and lesbian alcoholism, and becoming more involved in NALGAP's activities such as regional and national conferences and meetings. Both gay and non-gay people can become members and receive a quarterly newsletter.

International Advisory Council (IAC) for Homosexual Men and Women in Alcoholics Anonymous

P.O. Box 492
Village Station
New York, NY 10014

The IAC publishes a *World Directory of Gay/Lesbian Groups of Alcoholics Anonymous* which is updated periodically. This directory of meetings includes places, days, and times of meetings, and in some cases contact persons. It also publishes a newsletter and a list of *Gay/Lesbian Roundups*, which are conferences put on by members of A.A. and Al-Anon in many cities. These roundups may be helpful to clients for contacts with other sober people, information from workshops, and basic support.

National Lesbian and Gay Health Foundation (NLGHF)

P.O. Box 65472
Washington, DC 20035
(202) 797-3708

NLGHF is a nonprofit educational foundation that was organized to promote and increase awareness of lesbian and gay health concerns. Many professional gay/lesbian health organizations and caucuses support NLGHF and have taken part in and contributed to its seven national health conferences (since 1979), the *Health Directory*, and the *Sourcebook* (1984). NLGHF serves as a parent organization for the National Association of People with AIDS which provides a clearinghouse of information and resources for people with AIDS.

Gayellow Pages

Renaissance House
Box 292, Village Station
New York, NY 10014
(212) 674-0120

Many of the resources that counselors will need are listed in this publication. The national (including Canada) edition and the regional editions are updated frequently and provide a wealth of information including therapists, counseling centers, church groups, social and political organizations, health groups, hotlines, and some gay/lesbian meetings of A.A.

Gay/Lesbian Newspapers and Bookstores

All major cities and many smaller cities have one or more newspapers and bookstores that can provide information about local resources and gay/lesbian networks and activities. Newspapers and bookstores may be listed in local phone directories or in the *Gayellow Pages.*

Gay/Lesbian Switchboards

Most urban and some suburban areas of the country have switchboards that provide referral information for callers. They may have lists of gay-sensitive therapists, social groups, and A.A. meetings. Counselors need to familiarize themselves with these resources and provide them to clients. Many are listed in the *Gayellow Pages.*

Specialized Groups

There are support groups in many large urban areas for just about every special issue and problem imaginable. Most of these resources are listed in the *Gayellow Pages* or can be found through the local gay or lesbian switchboard or through the local Metropolitan Community Church (a gay church). Surprisingly, many places outside of large metropolitan areas also have support groups, and many members drive long distances to attend.

Listed below are some of the kinds of specialized groups that exist.

- Transsexual and Transvestite
- Lesbian and Gay Youth
- Married Gays
- Lesbian Mothers
- Gay Fathers
- Spouses of Gays
- Children of Gays
- Religious groups such as Catholic, Jewish, Episcopal
- Support groups for gay men and lesbians who are blind or deaf or otherwise physically challenged
- Political and social groups
- Gay/Lesbian ACOA groups

Specialized Treatment

In some areas there are specialized facilities and services for gay and lesbian people. Some of them are knowledgeable about alcoholism/chemical dependency; others are not. Ordinarily, these facilities and services can be located through the *Gayellow Pages*, the gay/lesbian switchboards, or NALGAP. In addition, NALGAP publishes a *Directory of Facilities and Services* that lists gay/lesbian-sensitive agencies and helping professionals.

Some of the established gay-sensitive or specifically gay/lesbian facilities and services around the country are listed below.

Inpatient

PRIDE Institute
14400 Martin Drive
Eden Prairie, MN 55344
(800) 547-7433
In MN (612) 934-7554

(Currently, this is the only gay/lesbian inpatient alcoholism/chemical dependency rehabilitation facility in the country. Several others are in the planning stages.)

Outpatient

Gay Council on Drinking Behavior
Whitman-Walker Clinic
2335 18th Street N.W.
Washington, DC 20009
(202) 332-5295

Chemical Dependency Program
1207 Pine Street
Seattle, WA 98101
(206) 682-4695

Gay & Lesbian Counseling Service
c/o 600 Washington Street, #219
Boston, MA 02111
(617) 542-5188

Women's Alcoholism Program
6 Camelia Avenue
Cambridge, MA 02139
(617) 661-1316

Montrose Counseling Center
900 Lovett, Suite 209
Houston, TX 77006
(713) 529-0037

Alcoholism Center for Women
1147 S. Alvarado Street
Los Angeles, CA 90006
(213) 381-7805

Gay & Lesbian Community Services Center
Box 38777/1213 N. Highland Avenue
Los Angeles, CA 90038
(213) 464-7400

18th Street Services
215B Market Street
San Francisco, CA 94114
(415) 861-4898

What About You?

As you have read through this book, hopefully you have learned a lot and gotten helpful information. In addition, your reading may have stirred up feelings of confusion or anxiety either about your sexual identity or your alcohol/drug use or abuse. This often happens to people and is not unusual or uncommon.

If you have some confusion or questions about sexual identity issues, you are not alone. We urge you to get help and support. You can talk to an accepting friend, call NALGAP, get in touch with a support group (check the *Gayellow Pages*), or talk to a non-homophobic therapist. But talk to *someone!*

If you are experiencing some confusion or anxiety about your alcohol or drug use or abuse, you are not alone. We urge you to get help and support. You can talk to an accepting friend, call the local A.A. Intergroup, call NALGAP, call the local Council on Alcoholism, check with the local gay/lesbian switchboard, call local treatment centers (many of them have out-patient programs), or talk to a non-homophobic alcoholism counselor. But talk to *someone!*

The material that follows may help you determine the extent and seriousness of your condition.

DIAGNOSIS OF ALCOHOLISM AND RELATED CHEMICAL DEPENDENCIES

(Chemical refers to all mood-altering drugs including ethyl alcohol.)

Ten Most Common Symptoms

1. *Preoccupation With Drinking*

    Do you ever look forward to the end of the day's work so that you can have a few drinks and relax?

    Do you sometimes look forward to the end of the week so you can drink the way you want to?

Does the thought of drinking sometimes enter your mind when you should be thinking of something else?

Do you feel the need of a drink at a particular time of the day?

2. *Increased Tolerance*

Have you found for the most part you can or could drink more than others?

Have you driven your friends home after drinking the same approximate amount because you were in better control than they were?

3. *Gulping Drinks*

Have you ever drunk right out of the bottle?

Do you usually drink fast out of a glass?

Do you usually order a double for the first one or two?

Have you frequently had a couple before going to a party or out?

4. *Use as a Medicine*

Have you drunk to calm your nerves?

Have you drunk to get to sleep or as an "eye opener"?

Have you drunk to relieve physical discomfort?

5. *Drinking Alone*

Have you ever stopped in a bar to have a couple by yourself?

Do you drink at home when no one else is there?

6. *Blackouts*

Have you ever had difficulty recalling how you got home?

Did you ever have trouble remembering, or not recall at all what happened the night before?

7. *Hiding Bottles*

Did you ever hide a bottle because you might need a drink?

Did you ever put a bottle in your pocket or in the glove compartment of your car?

8. *Non-Premeditated Drinking*

Have you stopped for one or two and had more than you planned?

Have you stopped for a drink when you planned to go directly home?

Are you the last one to leave the bar when you planned to go home early?

Have you usually drunk more than you know you should?

Is your drinking somewhat different from what you wish it was?

9. *Morning Tremors*

Have you had shakes or tremors of the hands after a night of drinking?

10. *Morning Drink*

Have you ever taken a drink in the morning to help you get over a hangover or the shakes or both?

Have you ever thought to yourself, you're not an alcoholic as long as you don't drink in the morning, and either force yourself not to give in before noon or rationalize you didn't get up until afternoon and that's not morning — and take one or two?

Admission to four or more symptoms is definite qualification for diagnosis of chemical dependency.

Remember *denial* is a major condition of alcoholism. If you have denied any of the above symptoms to another or yourself, it may cost you your home, job, or life. Admitting the problem is the first step to recovery.

Hopefully, these resources will assist clients — and you, if necessary.

EPILOGUE

As we look back over this book, we are struck by how rich and complex this subject truly is. We are also very aware of how difficult it is to capture or to do justice to the glorious complexity, diversity, and infinite variety of human experience. At best, we hope this book will serve as an introduction to some of the concerns and issues of gay and lesbian people, particularly those who are trying or wanting to recover from alcoholism or chemical dependency. In addition, we hope this book provides some understanding of and some practical suggestions and guidelines for counseling gay/lesbian alcoholics. In conclusion, we wish to make certain suggestions and comments.

This is just a book. And it is just one book. It is a start, but in order to more fully comprehend the complex issues gay people face and to become more comfortable working with them, you need to read other books and articles. Even more important, perhaps, is getting to know some gay people so you can personalize and begin to dissolve your stereotypes. It is important to look upon all of this as an ongoing educational process.

When you treat gay men or lesbians, you are not treating someone from Mars — though sometimes it feels like it. Keep in mind that you have your repertoire of skills, whose value and effectiveness do not lessen in the face of the unfamiliar experience or issues of gay/lesbian clients. Successful treatment relies much more on the constructive and accepting attitudes of the care givers than on their technical abilities.

Many people (both clients and treatment providers) confuse other problems with gay/lesbian identity/orientation issues. It is not uncommon for people to see such matters as sexual compulsiveness, gender identity problems, intimacy problems, sexual abuse, and psychiatric problems as sexual identity or orientation issues. Thus it becomes critically important to be able to make clear, nonjudgmental, sophisticated diagnoses and treatment plans. Just because a man is gay, for instance, does not mean he will or will not have emotional problems. He may be borderline and be gay. (He may also be alcoholic and act like a borderline personality.) Well-informed differential diagnoses are crucial.

Because of this need for sophisticated diagnostic skills and because such skills are always subject to bias and human error, we urge you to seek good, non-homophobic supervision and further training. It is also important to have staff support.

We believe all of us need to become advocates. Too often, people in the alcoholism field mistrust and resist other professionals working with people affected by alcoholism. But these professionals can learn about alcoholism and effectively treat people. Because gay men and lesbians have often received (and often continue to receive) such poor treatment, we need to encourage gay male and lesbian professionals to learn about alcoholism and ways to treat it. Our field needs the expertise and the spirit of these professionals.

We also need to raise our and others' consciousness about other minority groups and be advocates for them. The alcoholism field tends to be predominantly conservative, white, middle class, and male. The field needs many more blacks, gay men and lesbians, women, Latinos, native Americans, and Asians. And it needs them in every level of the system — administration, treatment, prevention, and education. We must make sure racism, classism, sexism, and homophobia are addressed, challenged, and eradicated everywhere.

Finally, we hope you will keep in mind that there are many "stories" — not just one or two. Kinsey created his now famous scale to express and accommodate the tremendous diversity of people's experiences. Too often, our culture views people in destructively narrow and limiting ways because is is so afraid of diversity and difference. Unfortunately, psychiatry and psychology tend to support such narrow perspectives by classifying according to normal versus abnormal. But the truth is, each of us has a story, and each of us wants to be accepted and responded to according to who we are as individuals. It is our responsibility, then, to make sure that we as treatment providers and concerned human beings recognize, respect, and celebrate each person's particular story.

Above all, we ask you to remember what a young, sober lesbian put into words:

> *When I was out there drinking myself to death, I thought drinking was a way of life and homosexuality was a disease. After I'd been sober awhile, I came to realize I'd gotten it backward. Alcoholism is the disease, and homosexuality is a way of life.*

BIBLIOGRAPHY

American Psychiatric Association, *Diagnostic and Statistical Manual of Mental Disorders* (Second Edition), Washington, DC, 1968.

Beatty, Roger, *Alcoholism and the Adult Gay Male Population of Pennsylvania*, unpublished master's thesis, University Park, PA, Pennsylvania State University, 1983.

Bell, Alan, and Martin S. Weinberg, *Homosexualities: A Study of Diversity Among Men and Women*, New York, Simon & Shuster, 1978.

Cass, Vivienne C., "Homosexual Identity: A Concept in Need of Definition," *Journal of Homosexuality*, 9 (2/3), 1984.

Cass, Vivienne C., "Homosexual Identity Formation: A Theoretical Model," *Journal of Homosexuality*, 4, 1979.

Cross, William E., "Discovering the Black Referent: The Psychology of Black Liberation," from *Beyond Black or White: An Alternate America*, V. J. Dixon and B. G. Foster, eds., Boston, Little, Brown & Co., 1971.

Fifield, Lillene, et al., *On My Way to Nowhere: Alienated, Isolated, Drunk*, unpublished project paper, Los Angeles, Office on Alcohol Abuse and Alcoholism, Los Angeles County Department of Health Services, 1975.

Ford, Clellan S., and Frank A. Beach, *Patterns of Sexual Behavior*, New York, Harper & Row, 1951.

Francoeur, Robert T., *Becoming a Sexual Person*, New York, John Wiley & Sons, 1982.

Goffman, Erving, *Stigma: Notes on the Management of Spoiled Identity*, Englewood Cliffs, NJ, Prentice-Hall, 1963.

Human Rights Foundation, Inc., *Demystifying Homosexuality: A Teaching Guide about Lesbians and Gay Men*, New York, Irvington Publishers, 1984.

Katz, Jonathan, *Gay American History: Lesbians and Gay Men in the U. S. A., A Documentary*, New York, Avon Books/Thomas Y. Crowell Co., Inc., 1976.

Kinsey, Alfred C., et al., *Sexual Behavior in the Human Male*, Philadelphia, W. B. Saunders Co., 1948.

Kinsey, Alfred C., et al., *Sexual Behavior in the Human Female*, Philadelphia, W. B. Saunders Co., 1953.

Klein, Fred, *The Bisexual Option*, New York, Berkley Books, 1978.

Klein, Fritz, "Are You Sure You're Heterosexual? Or Homosexual? Or Even Bisexual?" from *Forum* magazine, Dec. 1980.

Klein, Fritz, Barry Sepekoff, and Timothy J. Wolf, "Sexual Orientation: A Multi-Variable Dynamic Process," *Journal of Homosexuality*, 11 (1/2), Spring 1985.

Kus, Robert J., "From Grounded Theory to Clinical Practice: Cases From Gay Studies Research," in *From Grounded Theory to Clinical Practice: Qualitative Research in Nursing*, W. C. Chenitz and J. M. Swanson, eds., Menlo Park, CA, Addison-Wesley, 1986.

Kus, Robert J., "Stages of Coming Out: An Ethnographic Approach," from *Western Journal of Nursing Research* 7 (2), 1985.

Lohrenz, L. J., J. C. Connely, L. Coyne, and K. E. Spare, "Alcohol Problems in Several Midwestern Homosexual Communities," from *Journal of Studies on Alcohol*, 39, 1978.

National Association of Lesbian and Gay Alcoholism Professionals, *NALGAP Directory of Facilities and Services for Gay/Lesbian Alcoholics* (Revised Edition), New York, 1986.

National Association of Lesbian and Gay Alcoholism Professionals, *NALGAP Bibliography: Resources on Alcoholism and Lesbians/Gay Men* (Revised Edition), New York, 1987.

Ponse, Barbara, *Identities in the Lesbian World: The Social Construction of Self*, Westport, CT, Greenwood, 1978.

Rudy, David R., *Becoming Alcoholic: Alcoholics Anonymous and the Reality of Alcoholism*, Carbondale, IL, Southern Illinois University Press, 1986.

Saghir, M. T., E. Robins, B. Walbran, and K. E. Gentry, "Homosexuality: III. Psychiatric Disorders and Disability in the Male Homosexual," from *American Journal of Psychiatry*, *126*(8), 1970a.

Saghir, M. T., E. Robins, B. Walbran, and K.E. Gentry, "Homosexuality: IV. Psychiatric Disorders and Disability in the Female Homosexual," from *American Journal of Psychiatry*, *127*(2), 1970b.

Shakespeare, William, *The Tempest* (Act V, Scene 1, Lines 183-184), from *The Complete Works of Shakespeare*, G. L. Kittredge, ed., New York, Ginn and Company, 1936.

Weinberg, George, *Society and the Healthy Homosexual*, Garden City, NY, Anchor Press/Doubleday, 1972.

Weinberg, Martin S., and Colin J. Williams, *Male Homosexuals: Their Problems and Adaptations*, New York, Oxford University Press, 1974.

SUGGESTED READINGS

General Information

Adair, Casey, and Nancy Adair, eds., *Word is Out: Stories of Some of Our Lives*, New York, Dell Publishing Co., 1978.

Bell, Alan P., and Martin S. Weinberg, *Homosexualities: A Study of Diversity Among Men and Women*, New York, Simon & Schuster, 1978.

Berzon, Betty, and Robert Leighton, eds., *Positively Gay*, Millbrae, CA, Celestial Arts Publishing Co., 1979.

Boggan, E. C., M. G. Haft, C. Lister, J. P. Rupp, and T. S. Stoddard, *The Rights of Gay People* (Revised Edition), New York, Bantam Books, 1983.

Bullough, Vern L., *Homosexuality: A History*, New York, Meridian, New American Library, 1979.

Cass, V. C., "Homosexual Identity Formation: A Theoretical Model," from *Journal of Homosexuality*, 4(3), 1979.

Coleman, E., "Developmental Stages in the Coming Out Process," from *Journal of Homosexuality*, 7 (2-3), 1981-1982.

Gearhart, S., and W. R. Johnson, *Loving Women/Loving Men: Gay Liberation and the Church*, San Francisco, Glide Publications, 1974.

Human Rights Foundation, Inc., *Demystifying Homosexuality: A Teaching Guide About Lesbians and Gay Men*, New York, Irvington Publishers, Inc., 1984.

Jay, Karla, and Allen Young, *The Gay Report: Lesbians and Gay Men Speak Out About Sexual Experiences and Lifestyles*, New York, Simon & Schuster, 1979.

Kus, R. J., "Stages of Coming Out: An Ethnographic Approach," from *Western Journal of Nursing Research*, 7 (2), 1985.

Tripp, C. A., *The Homosexual Matrix*, New York, McGraw-Hill, 1975.

Weinberg, George, *Society and the Healthy Homosexual*, New York, St. Martin's Press, 1972.

Lesbians

Abbott, S., and B. Love, *Sappho Was a Right-On Woman: A Liberated View of Lesbianism*, New York, Stein & Day, 1972.

Klaich, D., *Woman + Woman: Attitudes Towards Lesbians*, New York, Simon & Schuster, 1974.

Lewis, L. A., "The Coming-Out Process for Lesbians: Integrating a Stable Identity," from *Social Work*, Sept./Oct. 1984.

Martin, D., and P. Lyon, *Lesbian/Woman*, New York, Bantam Books, 1972.

O'Donnell, M., K. Pollack, V. Leoffler, and Z. Saunders, *Lesbian Health Matters!* Santa Cruz, CA, Santa Cruz Women's Health Center, 1979.

Sisley, Emily L., and Bertha Harris, *The Joy of Lesbian Sex*, New York, Simon & Schuster, 1978.

Tanner, D. M., *The Lesbian Couple*, Lexington, MA, D. C. Heath & Co., 1978.

Vida, Ginny, ed., *Our Right to Love: A Lesbian Resource Book*, Englewood Cliffs, N.J., Prentice-Hall, Inc., 1978.

Gay Men*

Altman, Dennis, *Homosexual: Oppression and Liberation*, New York, Avon Books, 1971.

Clark, Don, *Loving Someone Gay*, New York, Signet Books, 1977.

Clark, Don, *Living Gay*, Millbrae, CA, Celestial Arts Publishing Co., 1979.

Levine, Martin P., *Gay Men: The Sociology of Male Homosexuality*, New York, Harper and Row, 1979.

---

*Our especial thanks to Michael Shernoff, CSW, ACSW, Chelsea Psychotherapy Associates, New York, NY, for his advice regarding citations for the sections on Gay Men and AIDS.

McWhirter, D. P., and A. W. Mattison, *The Male Couple: How Relationships Develop*, Englewood Cliffs, NJ, Prentice-Hall, 1984.

Silverstein, Charles, *Man to Man: Gay Couples in America*, New York, William Morrow & Co., 1981.

Walker, Mitch, *Men Loving Men: A Gay Sex Guide and Consciousness Book*, San Francisco, Gay Sunshine Press, 1985.

Bisexuals, Transsexuals, and Transvestites

De Cecco, J. P., and M. Shively, "Bisexual and Homosexual Identities: Critical Theoretical Issues," from *Journal of Homosexuality*, 9(2/3), 1983-1984.

Feinbloom, D. H., *Transvestites and Transsexuals: Mixed Views*, New York, Delta Publishers, 1976.

Klein, Fred, *The Bisexual Option*, New York, Berkley Books, 1978.

Klein, F., and T. J. Wolf, eds., *Two Lives to Lead: Bisexuality in Men and Women*, New York, Harrington Park Press, 1985.

Koranyi, Erwin K., *Transsexuality in the Male: The Spectrum of Gender Dysphoria*, Springfield, IL, Charles C. Thomas, 1980.

MacDonald, A. P., "Bisexuality: Some Comments on Research and Theory," from *Journal of Homosexuality*, 6(3), 1981.

Money, John, and Patricia Tucker, *Sexual Signatures: On Being a Man or a Woman*, Boston, Little, Brown & Co., 1975.

Parents and Youth

About Coming Out, New York, National Gay Task Force.

Alyson, Sasha, ed., *Young, Gay, and Proud*, Boston, Alyson Publications, 1980.

Fairchild, B., *Parents of Gays*, New York, Oscar Wilde Memorial Bookshop, 1975.

Fairchild, Betty, and Nancy Hayward, *Now That You Know: What Every Parent Should Know About Homosexuality*, New York, Harvest/Harcourt Brace Jovanovich, 1979.

Hanckel, Frances, and John Cunningham, *A Way of Love, A Way of Life: A Young Person's Introduction to What It Means to Be Gay*, New York, Lothrop, Lee & Shepard Books, 1979.

Gay Parents Support Packet, New York, National Gay Task Force.

Silverstein, Charles, *A Family Matter: A Parents' Guide to Homosexuality*, New York, McGraw-Hill, 1977.

Twenty Questions About Homosexuality, New York, National Gay Task Force.

Gay and Lesbian Alcoholics and Codependents

Anderson, S. C., and D. C. Henderson, "Working with Lesbian Alcoholics," from *Social Work*, 30(6), 1985.

Cirelli, D., and T. Rooney, "Treating the Gay and Lesbian Alcoholic," unpublished paper, available from NALGAP, 1982.

Finnegan, Dana G., and Emily B. McNally, "Alcoholism, Recovery, and Health: Lesbians and Gay Men," presented at the National Alcoholism Forum, Seattle, available from NALGAP, 1980.

Finnegan, Dana G., and Emily B. McNally, "How to See (and Help) the Invisible Lesbian Alcoholic," presented at NADC, Washington, DC, available from NALGAP, 1980.

Finnegan, Dana G., and D. Cook, "Special Issues Affecting the Treatment of Gay Male and Lesbian Alcoholics," from *Alcoholism Treatment Quarterly*, 1(3), 1984.

Nardi, P., "Alcohol Treatment and the Non-Traditional 'Family' Structure of Gays and Lesbians," from *Journal of Alcohol and Drug Education*, 27(2), 1980.

Swallow, J., ed., *Out From Under: Sober Dykes & Our Friends*, San Francisco, Spinsters, Ink., 1983.

The Way Back: The Stories of Gay and Lesbian Alcoholics, Washington, DC, Whitman-Walker Clinic, 1981.

Ziebold, Thomas, "Alcoholism and Recovery: Gays Helping Gays," from *Christopher Street*, Jan. 1979.

Ziebold, T. O., and J. E. Mongeon, eds., *Gay and Sober: Directions for Counseling and Therapy*, New York, Harrington Park Press, Inc., 1985.

General Counseling

Babuscio, Jack, ed., *We Speak for Ourselves: Experiences In Homosexual Counseling*, Philadelphia, Fortress Press, 1976.

Gonsiorek, John C., ed., *Homosexuality and Psychotherapy: A Practitioner's Handbook of Affirmative Models (Research on Homosexuality Ser.: No. 4)*, New York, The Haworth Press, 1982.

Hidalgo, H., T. L. Peterson, and N. J. Woodman, eds., *Lesbian and Gay Issues: A Resource Manual for Social Workers*, Silver Spring, MD, National Association of Social Workers, 1985.

Moses, A. Elfin, and Robert O. Hawkins, Jr., *Counseling Lesbian Women and Men: A Life-Issues Approach*, St. Louis, C. V. Mosby Co., 1982.

"Psychology and the Gay Community," ten articles from *Journal of Social Issues*. 34 (3), 1978.

Woodman, Natalie J., and Henry R. Lenna, *Counseling with Gay Men and Women: A Guide for Facilitating Positive Life-Styles*, San Francisco, Jossey-Bass, 1980.

Acquired Immune Deficiency Syndrome (AIDS)

Caputo, L., "Dual Diagnosis: AIDS and Addiction," from *Social Work*, July-August 1985.

Gay Men's Health Crisis, Inc., *Chance of a Lifetime*, (AIDS Prevention Video), available from GMHC, Dept. of Education, Box 274, 132 West 24th St., New York, NY 10011, 1986.

The Institute for Advanced Study of Human Sexuality, *Safe Sex in the Age of AIDS*, Secaucus, NJ, Citadel Press, 1985.

Jennings, Chris, *Understanding and Preventing AIDS: A Book for Everyone*, Cambridge, MA, Health Alert Press, 1985.

Korcok, M., *AIDS and Chemical Dependency: What the Treatment Community Needs to Know*, Pompano Beach, FL, Health Communications, Inc., 1985.

Mass, L., *Medical Answers About AIDS*, New York, GMHC, Dept. of Education, New York, 1986.

Palacios-Jiminez, L., and M. Shernoff, *Eroticizing Safer Sex: A Facilitator's Guide for AIDS Prevention Workshops*, New York, Gay Men's Health Crisis, 1986.

Smith, T. M., "AIDS and Substance Counseling With Gay Men," unpublished paper, San Francisco, available from NALGAP, April 1986.

Smith, T. M., "AIDS and Alcoholism: Denial Strikes Again," unpublished paper, San Francisco, available from NALGAP, 1985.

ENDNOTES

PART I

[1]Alfred C. Kinsey, et al., *Sexual Behavior in the Human Male* (Philadelphia, W. B. Saunders Co., 1948); Alfred C. Kinsey, et al., *Sexual Behavior in the Human Female* (Philadelphia, W. B. Saunders Co., 1953).

[2]Robert T. Francoeur, *Becoming a Sexual Person* (New York, John Wiley & Sons, 1982); Fred Klein, *The Bisexual Option* (New York, Berkley Books, 1978).

[3]Klein; Francoeur, p. 515.

[4]Klein; Alan P. Bell and Martin S. Weinberg, *Homosexualities: A Study of Diversity Among Men and Women* (New York, Simon & Shuster, 1978).

[5]Fritz Klein, Barry Sepekoff, and Timothy J. Wolf, "Sexual Orientation: A Multi-Variable Dynamic Process" (*Journal of Homosexuality, 11 no. 1/2*, Spring, 1985), pp. 35-49; Francoeur.

[6]*Ibid.*

[7]This is Francoeur's presentation and use of the Klein Grid.

[8]Clellan S. Ford and Frank A. Beach, *Patterns of Sexual Behavior* (New York, Harper & Row, 1951).

[9]Kinsey, *Sexual . . . Female*, and *Sexual . . . Male*.

[10]M. T. Saghir, E. Robins, B. Walbran, and K. E. Gentry, "Homosexuality: III. Psychiatric Disorders and Disability in the Male Homosexual" (*American Journal of Psychiatry, 126* (8), 1970a), pp. 1,079-1,086; M. T. Saghir, E. Robins, B. Walbran, and K. E. Gentry, "Homosexuality: IV. Psychiatric Disorders and Disability in the Female Homosexual" (*American Journal of Psychiatry, 127*(2), 1970b) pp. 147-154.

[11]Martin S. Weinberg and Colin J. Williams, *Male Homosexuals: Their Problems and Adaptations* (New York, Oxford University Press, 1974).

[12]Lillene Fifield, et al., *On My Way to Nowhere: Alienated, Isolated, Drunk*, unpublished project paper (Los Angeles, Office on Alcohol Abuse and Alcoholism, Los Angeles County Department of Health Services, 1975).

[13]L. J. Lohrenz, J. C. Connely, L. Coyne, and K. E. Spare, "Alcohol Problems in Several Midwestern Homosexual Communities" (*Journal of Studies on Alcohol*, 39,), pp. 1,959-1,963.

[14]Roger Beatty, *Alcoholism and the Adult Gay Male Population of Pennsylvania*, unpublished master's thesis (University Park, PA, Pennsylvania State University, 1983).

[15]Fifield.

[16]George Weinberg, *Society and the Healthy Homosexual* (Garden City, NY, Anchor Press/Doubleday, 1972).

[17]*Ibid.*

[18]Jonathon Katz, *Gay American History: Lesbians and Gay Men in the U. S. A., a Documentary* (New York, Avon Books/Thomas Y. Crowell Co., Inc., 1976).

[19]American Psychiatric Association, *Diagnostic and Statistical Manual of Mental Disorders* (Second Edition) (Washington DC, 1968).

[20]Human Rights Foundation, Inc., *Demystifying Homosexuality: A Teaching Guide About Lesbians and Gay Men* (New York, Irvington Publishers, 1984.)

PART II

[1]Human Rights Foundation, Inc., *Demystifying Homosexuality: A Teaching Guide about Lesbians and Gay Men* (New York, Irvington Publishers, 1984.)

[2]Erving Goffman, *Stigma: Notes on the Management of Spoiled Identity* (Englewood Cliffs, NJ, Prentice-Hall, 1963).

[3]David R. Rudy, *Becoming Alcoholic: Alcoholics Anonymous and the Reality of Alcoholism* (Carbondale, IL, Southern Illinois University Press, 1986); Goffman.

[4]Robert J. Kus, "From Grounded Theory to Clinical Practice: Cases From Gay Studies Research," in *From Grounded Theory to Clinical Practice: Qualitative Research in Nursing*, W. C. Chenitz and J. M. Swanson, eds. (Menlo Park, CA, Addison-Wesley, 1986); Robert J. Kus, "Stages of Coming Out: An Ethnographic Approach" (*Western Journal of Nursing Research 7* (2), 1985).

[5]William E. Cross, "Discovering the Black Referent: The Psychology of Black Liberation," from *Beyond Black or White: An Alternate America*, V. J. Dixon and B. G. Foster, eds. (Boston, Little, Brown, Inc, 1971), pp. 95-110.

[6]Vivienne C. Cass, "Homosexual Identity Formation: A Theoretical Model" (*Journal of Homosexuality*, 4, 1979), p. 219.

[7]Barbara Ponse, *Identities in the Lesbian World: The Social Construction of Self* (Westport, CT, Greenwood, 1978); Rudy.

[8]Cass, 1979 article.

[9]Cross.

[10]Cass, 1979 article; Vivienne C. Cass, "Homosexual Identity: A Concept in Need of Definition" (*Journal of Homosexuality*, 9 2/3, 1984), pp. 105-126.

[11]Cross, p. 104.

APPENDIX A

ADAPTED FROM AN *ORGANIZATION AUDIT: EVALUATING ORGANIZATIONAL ATTITUDES & PRACTICES FOR HOMOPHOBIA*

Developed by: Anthony Silvestre and Katherine Whitlock
Adapted by: Emily B. McNally and Dana G. Finnegan

Job Recruitment/Hiring/Promotion	YES	NO
Are job announcements sent to lesbian/gay agencies, organizations, such as NALGAP, and the media?	____	____
Are job candidates who are openly gay/lesbian, who are presumed to be gay/lesbian, or who have experience working with sexual minority concerns and populations discriminated against in any way, at any level, with regard to hiring and promotion?	____	____
Do informal guidelines exist regarding positions that openly lesbian/gay people would or would not be permitted to hold?	____	____
When candidates are interviewed for jobs, does your agency attempt to identify and screen out persons who are homophobic or who are not committed to ending discrimination against all minority-status persons?	____	____

The Organizational Environment for Employees

Does your agency's/organization's non-discrimination clause in its employment and service policies include sexual orientation (or sexual preference) and marital status?	____	____
If employees at your agency are unionized, does the union contract give equal protection to gay/lesbian members?	____	____

Is it generally accepted for lesbian and gay employees to be honest about their sexual orientation, both on the job and away from the job, without fear of sanctions or reprisals from management?   _____ _____

Are gay and lesbian staff ever formally or informally instructed to keep their sexual orientation hidden or quiet?   _____ _____

Is the agency environment such that some employees have chosen to be out of the closet as lesbians or gay men on the job?   _____ _____

Is the workplace generally supportive for sexual minority staff members?   _____ _____

Are "fag" or "dyke" jokes tolerated?   _____ _____

Are gay men, lesbians, or unmarried staff more socially isolated?   _____ _____

Does management defend lesbian/gay-supportive stands if such stands are questioned?   _____ _____

Have your employee benefits and leave time policies been analyzed to determine if they are equitable for single and gay/lesbian employees?   _____ _____

Are lesbians and gay men represented on your boards and on advisory and community committees?   _____ _____

Are gay and lesbian issues ever discussed at meetings of boards and committees? Are these concerns seen as important for all members to deal with?   _____ _____

Has your agency ensured the confidentiality of personnel records or other documents that contain information (whether implicit or explicit) about the sexual orientation of any staff members?   _____ _____

YES   NO

Professional Development
Has your agency's staff, ranging from management to line staff to maintenance workers, received in-service training on sexual minority persons? Has your board?   ____ ____

Provision of Services
Are announcements of services routinely sent to lesbian/gay agencies, organizations, and media?   ____ ____
Do your intake forms, other forms (including medical, social, sexual histories), treatment plans, brochures, and consumer publications assume the heterosexuality of your staff, clients, and donors?   ____ ____
Do your grant proposals and contracts for services show that your agency is serving a population that includes gay men and lesbians?   ____ ____
Does your agency state that lesbians and gay men are among the populations to be served?   ____ ____
Are your agency's confidentiality procedures adequate for protecting gay male and lesbian clients?   ____ ____
Do your agency's referral and resource lists include people/agencies with positive experience and expertise in working with sexual minority persons?   ____ ____
Are gay/lesbian meetings of A.A. and Al-Anon listed as choices for clients?   ____ ____
Are clients helped to attend these meetings if they choose to do so?   ____ ____
Are sexual minority issues relevant to either clients or staff addressed in intakes, supervision, and/or staff meetings?   ____ ____

127

Have your agency's programs and materials been analyzed and evaluated to identify areas where service/information do not adequately meet the needs of lesbians and gay men? Have corrective steps been taken?   ____   ____

When services are designed for family members or co-dependents, have the needs of same-sex couples been included?   ____   ____

At public hearings and in meetings with governmental officials and other public or private service providers, has your agency supported better services for the sexual minority community?   ____   ____

Is your agency prepared to meet the diverse needs of gay men and lesbians — including those of lesbian/gay youth; older lesbians and gay men; physically challenged gay men and lesbians; Third World lesbians and gay men?   ____   ____

Information Sharing and Community Relations

Do your agency's bulletin boards and literature racks include brochures, newsletters, flyers with information about gay and lesbian organizations, events, and services?   ____   ____

Does your agency's library contain books and articles by and about lesbians and gay men? Does it include books, articles, tapes by and about gay/lesbian recovering alcoholics?   ____   ____

Do films and audiotapes and lectures used in patient and community education include lesbians and gay men?   ____   ____

Do gay/lesbian groups of A.A. bring meetings into your agency?   ____   ____

Has your agency worked cooperatively and mutually with lesbian/gay groups in education efforts, fund-raising, and/or special community projects?   ____   ____

The Homosexual Alcoholic
A.A.'s Message of Hope
Gay men and lesbians will find hope in this pamphlet directed specifically to the problems of the homosexual alcoholic. It explains how A.A. groups for gays promote a sense of total identification and honesty while providing a shield of double anonymity. (16 pp.)
Order No. 1333B

Treating the Cocaine Abuser
by David E. Smith, M.D.,
Donald R. Wesson, M.D., editors
The country's leading experts on cocaine addiction have pooled the most recent information on treatment in this new book. Each chapter is devoted to a specific area of concern ranging from the medical and psychological complications of addiction, to support groups and recovery. (80 pp.)
Order No. 1464A

Each Day a New Beginning
The first daily meditation guide created by and for women involved in Twelve Step programs is now available in a durable hardcover gift edition. Since its initial publication in December 1982, over 400,000 women and men have used this collection of thoughts to welcome each day with new hope, strength, and courage. (400 pp.)

Order No. 1076 Softcover Edition

For price and order information, please call one of our Customer Service Representatives.

Hazelden ®
Educational Materials

Pleasant Valley Road
Box 176
Center City, MN 55012-0176

(800) 328-9000
(Toll Free. U.S. Only)
(800) 257-0070
(Toll Free. MN Only)
(800) 328-0500
(Toll Free. Film and Video Orders. U.S. Only)
(612) 257-4010
(Alaska and Outside U.S.)